THE
ARCHERS
OMNIBUS

THE ARCHERS OMNIBUS

The BBC's Official Companion to Radio's Most Popular Serial

JOCK GALLAGHER

BBC BOOKS

ACKNOWLEDGEMENTS

Because this omnibus comes from the endeavours of all those associated
with *The Archers* over many years there is simply not enough space to
acknowledge the contributions that so many people have made to the
everyday story of Britain's favourite countryfolk. I hope, therefore,
that all those not mentioned by name will accept grateful thanks for
their help and encouragement of my miserable authorship.

In particular, I appreciate the time taken by the very busy
writers and actors involved to provide me with biographical
details and appropriate photographs.

Because I have taken liberties with some of my friends in the
press, I would also like to specially acknowledge the newspapers from
which I have used or abused extracts, namely:– the *Daily Mail*, the
Daily Post (Liverpool), the *Daily Telegraph*, the *Guardian*, the
Independent, the *Kettering Evening Telegraph*, the *People*, the *Yorkshire
Post*, the *Shropshire Star*; and the magazines *Riva*, the *Listener*,
Country Living, *Country File*, *Good Fast Food*, the *Grocer*, *Stately
Homes and Gardens* and the *Sunday Express Magazine*.

I am also deeply grateful to Andra Heritage for her tireless
research and constant cheerfulness and to Juliet Lowe, whose secretarial
help and calmness in the face of word processor failure saved me from
heart failure.

Jock Gallagher.

PICTURE CREDITS

BIRMINGHAM POST & MAIL pages 71 *bottom* & 100; SUE CHAPMAN page 53
right; COUNTRY LIVING MAGAZINE page 20 (illustration by Paul Margiotta);
COVENTRY EVENING TELEGRAPH page 30 *left*; DAILY MAIL page 124;
PATRICK LICHFIELD page 10 *left*; PETER SIMPKIN page 65 *right*; SONY (UK)
LTD page 125; SPORT & GENERAL PRESS AGENCY page 14; UNIVERSAL
PICTORIAL PRESS front cover *centre left* & page 61 *left*; WILLOUGHBY
GULLACHSEN page 21 *bottom*; PAUL YATES page 47 *left*.

Published by BBC Books,
a division of BBC Enterprises Limited,
Woodlands, 80 Wood Lane, London W12 0TT
First Published 1990
© Jock Gallagher 1990
ISBN 0 563 36001 1

Set in 11/13 Goudy Roman by Butler & Tanner Ltd, Frome, Somerset
Printed and bound in Great Britain by Butler & Tanner Ltd, Frome, Somerset
Jacket printed by Belmont Press Ltd, Northampton

CONTENTS

CHAPTER ONE
THE ARCHERS, THEN AND NOW   6

CHAPTER TWO
THE VILLAGE OF AMBRIDGE   17

CHAPTER THREE
THE ACTORS AND THEIR CHARACTERS   36

CHAPTER FOUR
THE EDITORS   67

CHAPTER FIVE
THE WRITERS   78

CHAPTER SIX
IN THE MIDST OF LIFE…   84

CHAPTER SEVEN
THE LISTENERS STRIKE BACK   92

CHAPTER EIGHT
WHAT THE PAPERS SAY   105

CHAPTER NINE
EPISODE 10 000   113

CHAPTER TEN
ACCOLADES   123

THE ARCHERS, THEN AND NOW

I T IS VERY TEMPTING to try to claim that this Omnibus will tell you all you want to know about *The Archers*. The cliché rolls readily off the typewriter, and there's no doubt that it would look good on the cover and might make a superficially good selling point in the booksellers' displays. The truth, however, is that millions of fans already know more about the programme than can be dredged from my limited folk memory or culled from the filing cabinets that seem to fill the office.

My experience with the programme goes back 20 years and the files go back to the late 1940s, when Godfrey Baseley was still struggling to convince his masters that it was a good idea, but neither are a match for the real enthusiasts. No book could tell these listeners all they want to know. And there are an equal number of avid listeners who would hate to be told everything, anyway. They don't want to know that Phil and Jill Archer are going to . . . well, they don't want to know so I won't tell them, because perhaps more than any other, *The Archers* is the people's programme. The writers, editors and actors are only the beginning; the real magic happens when the listener switches on. That it still happens every week – for more than 7½ million listeners – is a tribute to those who so ingeniously created the programme and to the actors and production teams who have sustained it over these past 40 years.

The history of the programme's origins and early development has been recorded and published on many previous occasions and, though it will be touched on here, the main thrust of this book is the serial's more recent fortunes and how it has kept its position in British broadcasting.

As a result of continuous audience research, we know that, of the 7½ million regular listeners, about half listen to the daily episodes and one-third

At the grassroots . . . Godfrey Baseley's determination to make the script for The Archers *include regular visits to all those who made their living from the land. Even before the programme came on the air in 1951, he insisted on talking to countrymen like Maurice Jones to get his facts first hand.*

Putting on the style . . . Only Elizabeth Archer's wellies give away the fact that the country cousins have come to town for a spot of shopping. Jennifer Aldridge and Nigel Pargetter could pass muster as urbanites while the urbane Nelson Gabriel and the glamorous Caroline Bone would be at home anywhere.

to the Sunday omnibus edition. The others – about 16 per cent – probably listen twice a week. There is also a growing number of people who listen to the daily episodes *and* the omnibus. The *real* aficionados listen in during the week and try to second-guess the editor by working out which of the scenes will be cut to squeeze the five 15-minute daily episodes into the hour-long omnibus.

As well as the size of the audience, we also know quite a lot about its composition. For example, about 70 per cent are 'townies', and women listeners outnumber men by nearly two to one. We get an almost uniform spread across what are now known as the social grades, and something like 45 per cent are aged under 45.

Although less resistant to change than they once were, our regular listeners still have quite definite views about what they're prepared to go along with. They accept new characters because they bring fresh interest and they're reasonably happy with the way we portray women in the programme. Some see Elizabeth as a pain; Clarrie as too downtrodden; Jennifer as too naive; Peggy as too bossy and Jill as too nice. On the whole, however, they say there is a fair balance between Women's Institute and Women's Lib.

We have to be careful not to take change too far. When we were looking at ways of freshening up the programme a couple of years ago, we toyed with the idea of dropping 'Barwick Green' and introducing a new signature tune. Luckily we took the precaution of checking with the audience first: only 2 per cent didn't have a view on the subject; 6 per cent thought it was quite a good idea; another 12 per cent said they weren't keen; and a thumping 80 per cent told us very emphatically to leave well alone. Whose silly idea was it anyway?

That same 80 per cent tell us that we've got the balance of farming interests just about right and that the scripts do give a fair portrayal of village life in the 1990s. The one hint we keep getting is that many listeners would like the programme to remain just a little removed from the real world . . . but that's not as easy as it sounds. If you step back too far, you can end up slipping into sheer fantasy or, even worse, becoming hopelessly nostalgic, constantly hankering after yesterday. Our answer is to try to keep a balance between all these extremes, and it's true that the language in Ambridge is less violent than you'll hear in many school playgrounds, the plots are hardly in the *Miami Vice* vein and the pace of the action is less hurried than in trendier soaps.

One of the dangers constantly faced by *The Archers* team, as by many other programme-makers, is that we might start believing our own publicity. and then our audience research will only tell us the things we want to hear. It's always useful, therefore, to get corroborative evidence from independent sources.

Writing in the *Observer*'s media column in May 1989, Deborah Vogler reported on what she called 'a new wireless era' and referred to Radio 4's quest for a younger audience. She said that during a tour of Britain's universities, the Controller (Michael Green) had found that *The Archers* was cult listening among students. She also noted that while *Citizens* (aimed at younger listeners) attracted a healthy under-forties audience, there was 'ironically, a larger younger audience for *The Archers*, which cleverly bridges all age groups'. A couple of months later, the specialist magazine, *PR Week*, reported a survey by the Media Business Group showing that *The Archers* was second only to the 8am News in the Radio 4 popularity stakes.

In the early days the cynics suggested that the initial success of the programme had as much to do with luck as good judgement. They argued that *The Archers* started at a time when the British public were looking for something to alleviate the greyness of the post-war recovery period, and the programme gave people the vicarious pleasure of regular visits to the countryside and some metaphorical fresh air.

Such arguments could not be used today. The media explosion has created more entertainment opportunities than anyone could ever have imagined; television, commercial television, colour television, cable television, satellite television, home videos, records, cassettes and compact discs all vie for our attention.

On the radio front there are the three other BBC networks, BBC local radio, commercial local radio and now community radio. Even within Radio 4, *The Archers* has to hold its own against other soap operas such as *Citizens*, *Crown House* and, more recently, *The House* (created by a former *Archers* writer). To win and hold an audience in this climate requires enormous skill, energy and commitment. And down the years, the *Archers* writers, actors and producers have met each new challenge with confidence and style.

Through all the ups and downs, the lowest point was undoubtedly in the late sixties and early seventies when television was enjoying huge popularity, radio audiences were diminishing and morale within the programme had been shot to pieces. It's no secret that when I was appointed, in 1970, I was given the job of sorting out these problems or taking the programme off the air. The fact that it's still going suggests that, at the very least, we stopped the rot in the seventies. The road to full recovery, however, was long and arduous.

The nature of the BBC hierarchy is that while I had the responsibility, I didn't have any real hands-on control and my main task was to assemble the right calibre of staff to do the job. I was very lucky, particularly in the key appointments of successive editors. Malcolm Lynch provided the jolt that helped us shake off the inertia; Charles Lefeaux applied a steadying hand; William Smethurst introduced a new wit and style; and Liz Rigbey had a special integrity in rural affairs. Each has made a

I want to tell you a storyline . . . Editor Ruth Patterson chairs the monthly script meeting, flanked by secretary Joy Tonkin, agricultural adviser Tony Parkin and producer Niall Fraser. During the meeting, which lasts most of the day, Ruth and the writers devise the plots and character twists that will keep listeners engrossed through·another 20 episodes.

contribution that seems to me to be precisely what was needed at the various times. Ruth Patterson, the current editor, has an abundance of youthful energy and tenacity, the qualities needed for the next stage of development.

Despite all our work in the seventies, there was little perceptible change in the size of the audience and it was only as we moved into the eighties that our figures started improving. William Smethurst was the first editor to acknowledge that *The Archers* was indeed a soap opera. Earlier regimes had resisted the description because they thought it demeaning; William saw it as a social comedy in which wit was an essential ingredient. He introduced new characters like the Grundys, Nigel Pargetter, Clarrie Larkin and Mrs Antrobus, and he persuaded the writers to conceive their

storylines in terms of a 60-minute drama instead of five single episodes and that improved the quality of the scripts and gave the serial a more cohesive form.

With a better product (one which we were again proud enough to sell), William and I found we shared the philosophy that there was no point in having a great programme if the world didn't know about it. So we set out to make sure it did; and if the audience wouldn't come to us, we would go to the audience. William devised a roadshow that travelled around the country giving people a chance not only to meet their favourite characters but also to act alongside them with special scripts.

Radio 4 was also going out and about, and *The Archers* would be part of the entertainment at each major venue. In Norwich, for example, we took over a small theatre to do a question-and-answer session we thought would last about an hour. It over-ran by 2 hours and none of us got any supper that night.

Meet the wife . . . Mark Hebden finally marries into the dynastic Archer family when he takes Shula as his blushing bride.

On the horns of a dilemma . . . Eddie Grundy fans John Peel and John Walters found they had to put up with yuppie Nigel Pargetter (who naturally insisted on a glass of wine) before they could slurp ale with their hero. This was not the night Eddie was sick in the piano at The Bull . . . but he did come close.

We designed T-shirts (that urged people to 'Cultivate *The Archers*') and sweatshirts for the Hollowtree Playboy Club (Hollowtree is, of course, Brookfield's pig unit and Playboy was the prize pig). Later came a car-sticker which used the slogan, '*The Archers* do it twice a day and for an hour on Sundays', and proved to be a bestseller.

A stage show was written and produced. And when it played for four weeks at the Watermill Theatre in Newbury, it was a complete sell-out. It featured nine of the cast (ten if you include Jack Woolley's dog, Captain) and was uniquely set in the theatre (doubling as Ambridge Village Hall), outside on the river bank (the village green) and on a neighbouring farm (Grange Farm).

Brian Aldridge and Elizabeth Archer did a show-stopping song-and-dance routine; Jack Woolley organised a wellie-wanging contest to see who could throw the green wellie furthest; and Joe Grundy was nearly killed when a huge bale of hay fell on him. There was a real-beer tent, Mr Snowy's ice-cream van, a maypole and even a Red Cross ambulance to fetch poor Joe from the farm.

The show was so successful that it transferred to London . . . not quite to the West End but to a huge marquee in the shadow of the old Battersea power station. (Sadly, it didn't enjoy the same success there, despite including Mark and Shula's wedding celebrations.)

Slowly the audience figures started to increase and we turned up the marketing pressure, seldom missing an opportunity to promote the programme. When the Young Tories complained about something they regarded as left-wing propaganda, we turned up at their annual conference in Blackpool with loyal (sic) blue car-stickers that said 'Conserve Ambridge'. Then, just to stay even-handed, we gave the left 'Nuclear-free Ambridge' buttons. A collector's bone-china plate, a selection of miniature cottages and farmhouses, an illustrated map, a computer game and several books all came off the production line with varying degrees of success. Members of the cast were even chosen as models for an upmarket knitting catalogue. We also licensed a tour operator to run a series of theme weekends and these proved popular enough for us to extend the licence and allow Heart of England Country Tours to re-introduce them in 1989.

Listeners now started to come out of the closet and we learned that the growing millions included a sprinkling of celebrities. Wendy Richards, Zandra Rhodes, Adrian Juste, Captain Sensible, Sue Lawley, Glenys Kinnock, Terry Wogan, Ned Sherrin, Bob Hoskins and the Duke of Westminster were among those who confessed their addiction and even the Queen Mother's private secretary visited the studios to watch the recording and meet the actors.

Suddenly we also had the Eddie Grundy phenomenon. Eddie had been created to add a touch of comic relief and Trevor Harrison's characterisation of a potential villain, who was never quite crooked enough to get into real trouble, was so successful that Eddie became a folk anti-hero. A group of enthusiasts (including Radio 1 disc jockey, John Peel) formed an Eddie Grundy Fan Club which still meets regularly and has its own mini-industry selling Grundy paraphernalia. We gave the world Grundy pork-scratchings – said to be a delicacy in some parts of the country! – and no fewer than four Eddie Grundy records have been released upon the innocent and unsuspecting public.

Our constant search for writers became slightly easier and we were able to tempt one of Britain's best novelists, Susan Hill, to join the script team. Meanwhile, actors such as Frank Middle-mass, Don Henderson, Angela Thorne and Richard Griffiths joined the cast. Ted Moult, perhaps then the best-known farmer in Britain, asked to audition when we were looking for an actor to become the fourth Dan Archer. Frank Middlemass got the role but Ted gave such a lovely, warm performance that we created the part of Bill Insley for him. In addition, former newsreader-turned-documentary-maker, Angela Rippon, made an appearance in Ambridge, and Pamela Armstrong played opposite Jill Archer in her own *Pamela Armstrong Show* on BBC1.

When he was planning the Mark and Shula wedding and thinking about photographers, William Smethurst decided to start at the top. To our surprise and delight, Lord Lichfield readily agreed to fit the assignment into his busy schedule. His photographs got us on to the front cover of the *Radio Times* for the first time in many years. But the great coup (the one that all the other programmes still envy) was when William Smethurst persuaded Princess Margaret to become the first member of the Royal Family to take part in a soap opera.

All these exploits and events were duly chronicled in the press, and the *Guardian* letters page suffered (or, should I say, benefited) from an astonishing rash of correspondence about the programme. The rash spread to most of the other quality papers and magazines.

Even radio, usually anxious to avoid charges of self-interest, sat up and took notice. Barry Norman was commissioned to write and present a special feature about *The Archers* and Liz Rigbey started what we hope will become something of a tradition by producing an *Archers* Christmas special for Radio 4 in 1987. Just as television puts all its major programmes into the Christmas bill of fare, so Liz did with *The Archers*. She created a programme from the archives and, with so many memorable scenes from the past, it proved very popular. It was made into a double cassette and became one of the best-selling items in the BBC Radio Collection of classics. A second cassette has since been produced.

When the BBC in the Midlands and BBC Books combined to run a series of celebrity dinners in 1988, Liz and I launched the first event and

Joining the celebrities . . . Former editor Liz Rigbey and Jock Gallagher team up to carry The Archers *flag at the first BBC in the Midlands celebrity dinner in April 1988. They had the unenviable task of paving the way for Barry Norman and David Dimbleby.*

Mean and moody . . . Eddie Grundy plays his grandfather in the 1988 Christmas production of To the Victor the Spoils *(adapted for radio from the first novel in* The Archers Saga*).*

shared the platform with Barry Norman and David Dimbleby. We also kept up the literary momentum. Liz produced the first *Archers* quiz book, with such questions as: 'At Brookfield, lambing starts at the end of February. So when does tupping take place?' And I produced *The Archers Saga* in the form of three novels: *To the Victor the Spoils*; *Return to Ambridge*; and *Borchester Echoes*. The first book was adapted for radio by Peter Mackie and when it was produced as a 90-minute Christmas special for Radio 4, the casting included Trevor Harrison playing Eddie Grundy's grandfather!

There was another first for the programme in 1988, when Australia's leading lady, Dame Edna Everage, let it be known that she might consider an appearance in 'your lovely little soapy thing'. In the event, Barry Humphries invited Lynda Snell to join him on stage during one of his live shows. We recorded the spectacle – of Mrs Snell getting her

comeuppance – and later broadcast it within *The Archers*. When reporters, first from the *Sunday Express* and later the *Sunday Telegraph*, made appearances in the programme, we had to call a halt lest we were inundated with other requests for special treatment.

Austin Rover's advertising agents spotted the pulling power of *The Archers* and put it to commercial use in launching the new Montego Countryman car in 1988. In their glossy, full-colour advertisements in most of the national magazines (including our own *Radio Times*), they showed their new hi-tech car alongside bales of straw, pitchforks, waxed jackets and green wellies. The legend read: 'Ambridge goes Silicon.'

The editor was not amused because the company had not asked for permission to use the association with the programme (which, in any case, we would not have given). Other companies have since sought endorsements for a wide range of products from chocolates to butter but the licensing arrangements made through BBC Enterprises Ltd are stringent enough to protect us from any unwelcome advances.

Part of the programme's current popularity may well be linked with increasing awareness of Green issues in Britain. The Prime Minister is clearly aware of the mood of the country and in an exclusive interview with Terry Tavner, editor of *Chat* magazine, Mrs Thatcher sought the help of television's soap opera producers in advancing the cause of conservation. To quote her words:
I think they could do something and I'm sure this is in the minds of some scriptwriters. Sometimes I notice, listening to **The Archers***, that you will find some of these messages coming across, like: 'You don't do such a thing because it will harm the environment . . .' I think they will get a tremendous response.*

So glad you could come . . . Who else but Lynda Snell could imagine that she had got the better of Dame Edna during a 1988 encounter at a theatre in Newcastle?

Nice as it is to have the Prime Minister registered as one of our voters, it's a little worrying to have her political endorsement . . . and when it comes from both sides, it's even more difficult to handle!

Not to be outdone by the government, the Labour Party also discovered that it approved of what we were up to. When the party launched its 'Labour Listens' campaign in 1988, the Shadow Minister for Agriculture, Dr David Clark, said a good starting point for senior Labour leaders would be to tune in to *The Archers*. 'That radio programme constantly reminds us that the problems of poverty and deprivation exist in many pockets of the country.'

On the other side of the social divide, the Country Landowners' Association (CLA) turned to us for help in convincing people that they weren't involved with anything that would harm the rural environment. When the Ramblers' Association claimed that its members and other walkers were endangered by the 30 000 tons of pesticides used on the land each year, the CLA said it was 'emotional clap-trap' and that if anyone wanted to

know about the strictness of the spraying practice code that operates in Britain, they should listen to *The Archers*: 'Only recently Phil Archer failed his spraying test and was embarrassed by the fact that Ruth, one of his young workers, passed. There are pretty strict controls, not only on spraying methods but on the chemicals used.'

The farmers themselves jumped on the bandwagon when they commissioned Research Surveys of Great Britain to do a public opinion poll about their popularity with the general public, using Ambridge farmers as role models. Not surprisingly: 'The majority view of the typical farmer is of a Phil Archer stereotype – a highly regarded member of society for whom farming is a way of life.'

Closer to home, the farmers and other villagers from Hanbury, the village on which Godfrey Baseley modelled Ambridge, were quick to exploit the connection when they were threatened by a development plan to create a new satellite village in the area. That's a story which looks like running for several more years.

Overseas farmers are also being encouraged to do it the Ambridge way. If imitation is the sincerest form of flattery, Godfrey Baseley should blush at the contents of a United Nations discussion document published in Rome in 1987. It urges Third World countries to consider setting up their own versions of *The Archers* as a way of resolving some of the huge food-growing problems they face. The author of the 30-page document, *Education Through Entertainment*, is Colin Fraser, a Rome-based agriculturist who made a long study of *The Archers* and its impact on British farmers over the years, on behalf of the UN's Food and Agriculture Organisation.

He describes Godfrey as 'a born development communicator of inimitable talent and imagination', and draws parallels between rural England in the late 1940s (when the programme was conceived) and many areas of developing countries today. In his paper, Mr Fraser analyses the

Prime Minister meets prime beef . . . or nearly! This animal was the champion dairy cow at the Dairy Festival in London in 1961. Harold Macmillan took the opportunity of exchanging agricultural gossip with Monte Crick (second from the right) who was then playing Dan Archer.

programme's genesis, the concepts behind it and, most importantly for his readers, the success it has achieved:

So realistically speaking, could the approach be replicated today in a Third World country? There is no doubt the talent exists and it would only be a question of channelling it in the right direction and paying for it. This raises the issues of resources and their allocation.

Few radio stations have enough vehicles for travelling into the countryside, for example, and many are short of studio time. Hitherto, few broadcasting authorities have given any real importance to rural programming which is viewed as a poor sister compared to news, culture and sports . . . not to mention politics.

So, in fact, we are back to the old issue of the prestige of the rural sector and the resources devoted to its interests. If a policy decision were made to shift resources for the production of a dramatised rural service, it could, no doubt, be done and done well in many countries.

Mr Fraser then compares the advantages of using radio rather than television (generally regarded as having greater impact) for such a programme. He reasserts the well-known philosophy that the pictures are better on the radio (thanks to listeners' fertile imaginations) but then adds the practical note that it is also much cheaper because you don't have to arrange expensive film shoots. Finally he asks:

Is it really beyond developing countries to enliven their rural radio programming and to steal a few leaves out of Baseley's book . . . even if they cannot grab and use the whole book? There must surely be lessons in the experience of **The Archers** *that could be applied to making entertainment a vehicle for learning in many parts of the world.*

Any day now, we should hear about a froth of agricultural soap operas all round the developing world!

Education was clearly also in the mind of the officer in charge of the Gurkha Brigade in Hong Kong when he wrote to us a few years ago. He wanted to know if it was all right if he used *The Archers* to help teach the Gurkhas colloquial English. We agreed, of course, and had visions of lots of Gurkhas going around brandishing their fearsome knives and wishing everyone 'Morning all' in a Tom Forrest accent! That letter was also a reminder that the programme is still heard on all the British Forces broadcasting stations around the world. When Ambridge's Terry Barford joined the army, we got a surprising number of letters from soldiers identifying with him.

We received another reminder of our military fans when the late Gwen Berryman went to Buckingham Palace to receive the MBE – awarded for her long service in the part of Doris Archer. The duty regiment was the Scots Guards. Still suffering the after-effects of two strokes, Gwen was in a wheelchair. As she was pushed towards the main entrance, a young subaltern from the Guards came skidding across the courtyard and threw up an impeccable salute. A startled Gwen, assuming that everyone arriving for the investiture ceremony was accorded the same treatment, smiled broadly and gave what she thought was a regal wave of acknowledgement.

When she realised the full significance of the greeting, the smile faded and Gwen was moved to tears. The officer presented his compliments and, to a ragged version of 'Barwick Green' from the young men behind him, said he had been asked to thank her on behalf of the whole regiment for all the pleasure she and the rest of the cast had given the guardsmen while they'd been stationed in Berlin. 'The men listened to your programme every night. It was their link with home,' he said . . . and many of the soldiers in the background were from Glasgow.

Three other members of *The Archers* team have made that same trip to Buckingham Palace to be honoured by the Queen . . . Tony Shryane (who had at that time produced the programme for ten years), Norman Painting (who had played Phil for 25 years) and Chriss Gittins (who had played Walter Gabriel for 30 years).

Lest I give the impression that it's been an easy climb back to popularity, it may be worth logging some of the setbacks and savage blows we've had to overcome along the way.

As you will read later in the book, death is one of the inevitabilities of a long-running series and although we have learned to cope with it in reasonably professional terms, the loss of each member of the team still leaves the rest of us numb and unnerved. Never more so than when the gentle Fiona Mathieson and the ebullient Ted Moult killed themselves within 12 months of each other (see Chapter Six).

Retirements and resignations are also par for the course but when William Smethurst resigned as editor to take up his job as executive producer of Central Television's *Crossroads*, he took most of the staff and writers (and two of the cast) with him. William took considerable pains to let me know his intentions but while that was helpful, it still created massive problems for us. Editors and writers are not always waiting around to be asked to join *The Archers*.

It was Liz Rigbey who faced the worst of the traumas. When she became editor in 1986, she inherited the empty office from William and worked like a demon to repair the damage but no sooner had she got her team together than several of its members were struck down by hepatitis. The irony was that the bug struck at a lunch given by radio's managing director, David Hatch, to celebrate the programme's winning the coveted Sony Gold Award. Liz, her assistant producer and four members of the cast were affected, and their enforced absence caused considerable rewriting of the scripts and even greater strain on our already stretched resources.

When 1989 saw the deterioration of industrial relations in Britain, *The Archers* had no immunity from the rash of strikes that affected the country. Liz Rigbey's introduction to her new job may have been traumatic, but Ruth Patterson arrived in May 1989, and immediately had to face the nerve-jangling scheduling problems caused first by the broadcasting unions' series of snap strikes and then by the railwaymen's one-day stoppages. Some days she had studio and staff but no cast because they couldn't get to Pebble Mill without the trains. On other days she had the actors but no studios because the BBC staff had gone on strike.

We know that there are bound to be further difficulties in the future and that the programme may be overtaken somewhere along the way by a different kind of radio experience offering greater allure than the rural idyll. From where we stand at the moment, however, with more than 10 000 episodes behind us, it is becoming easier to view problems as mere challenges. These are not days of nervousness and insecurity. There are no signs of the bailiff's men waiting to foreclose.

One of the great things about working on the programme today is the sheer pleasure most people get out of what they're doing. The hours are long, the conditions sometimes difficult, the boss all-too-often crabby, but at the end of each production day, with a few more episodes safely recorded, there's a feeling of satisfaction in the air.

The programme is acknowledged by listeners and our professional peers alike. We won the Sony Gold Award (the premier prize for an outstanding contribution to broadcasting) in 1987 and in 1988, after being among the most popular attractions at the BBC Radio Show, the programme was voted not only the best drama but also the best contemporary programme by readers of the *Daily Mail*. Like those who have already taken the fear out of being 40, the youngest editor and youngest production team the programme's ever had are set to sail through our 40th anniversary in 1991 as comfortably as Jane Fonda keeps in trim.

And we can look further ahead with confidence towards the year 2001 – the programme's golden jubilee – with visions of our own space odyssey: a different sort of space . . . green space, inner not outer space, to contemplate the finer things of life . . . a different sort of odyssey . . . taking a quieter route than the rat-race, travelling at a speed where we can think and reflect. That way, we might go on satisfying those listeners who prefer us to be that bit removed from the real world.

— CHAPTER TWO —
THE VILLAGE OF AMBRIDGE

AMBRIDGE IS NOT AN especially big village. The census says it had a population of just 360 when last counted but that was a good few years ago and, such is the nature of a small, rural community, nobody is quite sure about today's numbers. In truth, no one cares much about statistics anyway. Everybody knows everybody else and that's all that matters.

There are some people who would say that it isn't really a village at all. One of the new, Green lobby groups insists that to qualify as a village it would have to boast ten vital amenities: community hall, church, pub, post office, shop, school, housing for all incomes, social activities for all age groups, local jobs and public transport.

Ambridge falls short on at least two counts (no school and no buses) and there are locals who would question whether there are jobs and houses for ordinary folk. Eddie Grundy and his cronies and Elizabeth Archer would also raise an argument or two about the social life in Ambridge. But as to whether or not it qualifies as a village in the Greens' eyes, no one is much bothered. These particular countryfolk care even less about lobby groups than they do about statistics and they reckon they've been around long enough to know a village when they see one!

Village or not, Ambridge stands right in the heart of Borsetshire, 6 miles south of the county town of Borchester, and halfway between Felpersham and the nearest railway station at Hollerton Junction. As you approach along the B3980 road from Borchester, Lakey Hill rises on your left just before you reach the centre of the village and at the top, some 450 feet up, you'll find an ideal vantage point to view the sprawling layout of the tiny community.

The local GP, Dr Matthew Thorogood, in cynical mood, once said it was the best place to spy on your neighbours. He could be right. You can see everything from here . . . Mrs Antrobus walking her dogs, Clarrie Grundy pegging out her father-in-law's longjohns, Phil Archer driving his tractor across Brookfield's broad acres, Lynda Snell on her seemingly endless mission to conserve everything in sight and Dave Barry, hellbent on promotion, keeping a policeman's eye on the rougher elements in the community.

From the hilltop, the view wouldn't exactly gladden the heart of a modern planner. It's a careless hand that has dotted farmhouses, cottages and a few country houses around the green fields on either side of the River Am as it lazily meanders along the valley. Up here, you can look down on the village through the early-morning mist or the late-afternoon heat-haze – or, some might say, through rose-tinted spectacles – and see an idealised, timeless community with pleasantly blurred edges.

To some extent, you can measure the success of the conservationists by what you don't see from up here. There's very little development that's out of character with these particular green acres. As yet, Ambridge is untouched by the cruel march of time. Despite continuous threats, there are none of the ugly scars caused by housing estates and new roads. The latest attempt to build a new feeder road from the Borchester bypass towards Ambridge failed through lack of funds, though Lynda Snell will tell you it was because of the stout opposition of the villagers.

Many rural areas may be facing what's been described as 'a development disaster' as more and more people decide to move out of crowded towns and cities. Borsetshire planners, however, are determined to resist the pressures on their village communities. They belong to the National Society for County Planning Officers which last year produced a plan called 'Caring for the Countryside', calling for more co-operation between councils and the increasingly powerful voluntary conservation groups.

She knew they were coming so she baked lots of cakes . . . but then Jill Archer always does exactly the right thing. Sunday afternoon tea brings the family together and there's still plenty left when Brian Aldridge drops in unexpectedly.

The pressures mustn't be underestimated, of course. There is certainly an unprecedented demand for land to build new roads, more homes, out-of-town shopping centres, industrial estates and even giant leisure complexes. In some areas, farmers and landowners have not been slow in making bids to convert their land to these alternative uses. But not here. Apart from Philip Archer who sold a small parcel of land for a minor barn-conversion development, the farmers around Ambridge have so far resisted the temptation to cash in on this trend and have refused to sell agricultural land to the developers for huge profits. Encouraged by the enlightened attitude at County Hall, they believe that any building would be a serious encroachment into the countryside and the very open spaces that the townspeople say they want to enjoy. As Lynda Snell might say, long may their altruism survive!

On Lakey Hill, it's easy to forget about such problems and to see only the rural idyll. At this distance from the hurly-burly, you can believe tomorrow doesn't have to catch up with Ambridge and destroy the dream. Felpersham, Borchester,

The Archers of Brookfield . . . Mum, Dad and the kids pose for a rare family photograph, on the steps of St Stephen's, at David's wedding. With David and Shula married, Kenton living in Borchester and Elizabeth rushing around playing the journalist, Phil and Jill don't see a great deal of their offspring these days.

Gerry's building . . . St Stephen's Church is now in the care of the Reverend Gerry Buckle who is less concerned with the fabric of the ancient building than the well-being of his flock . . . not that the flock always appreciate it!

Worcester and Birmingham may be geographically close but, emotionally, they're light-years away.

As your eye scans the landscape, there's little to stop the mind drifting back to bygone days when the air was cleaner and quieter; when the sweet smell of muck-spreading was the closest you came to pollution and the only sound to be heard was the humming of the ploughman as he and his horse spent a whole day ploughing a single acre.

Those yesterdays were days of contrasts, though. A beneficent squire would pay his men even for the time they spent in church . . . but throw their widows out of tied cottages almost as soon as their husbands were dead and buried. Milking had to be done by an unearthly five o'clock in the morning to get the milk to the towns by six . . . but those who met the deadline earned an extra penny per gallon.

Then, the fields around Ambridge would have been much smaller and they would have been neatly boxed in by row upon row of hedges. Times have changed and the splendid patchwork of farms that represents the lifeblood of the villagers is now much more open, with only the occasional fence to break up the pattern.

Not surprisingly, it's St Stephen's Church that dominates the skyline as you look southwards, down over the village. The parish church lies on the far side of Ambridge on the Waterley Cross road. It's built on the site of a seventh-century St Augustine church and the architecture is said to be a mixture of the Saxon, late-Norman, early-English and perpendicular styles.

You can't tell from this distance but the bell tower has a 6-inch list, probably because (as they discovered in the early 1970s when the bells crashed to the ground) it has no regular foundations. However that doesn't seem to worry the present vicar, the Reverend Jerry Buckle. He arrived in January 1989, to replace Richard Adamson, and has been described as a 'muscular' Christian, more concerned about his role in the community than about the fabric of the church.

Some of his sermons have certainly raised local eyebrows because of their political content, and the Reverend Buckle was none too popular when he spoke in favour of a bypass which, he felt, might bring starter homes for local young people in its wake. At one stage, he was even considering selling off more of the glebeland for rural housing development and that also caused consternation among certain members of the Green brigade.

On the other hand, Mr Buckle (who, it transpired, left the army because of his pacifism) showed considerable Christian charity by sharing the vicarage with Clive Horrobin, his girlfriend, Sharon, and their baby daughter. There are, however, several members of his flock who think he's being taken for a ride by the young couple. These days, when the bells of St Stephen's ring out on Sunday mornings, they call some of the faithful a mite uncertainly to worship.

If you let your eye drop from St Stephen's church tower, it should catch the black-and-white

timbered local pub, parts of which are said to date back to the seventeenth century. The Bull is the more popular of the village's two pubs (the other is the recently refurbished Cat and Fiddle), probably because of its prime position in the knot of cottages and houses around the village green. Now run by Sid Perks, it's actually owned by Mrs Peggy Archer, who last year turned down a £750000 offer from the Borchester and Borset Hoteliers. They wanted to turn it into a carvery. While they were delighted that the pub was staying in local hands, most of the villagers were surprised that Mrs Archer hadn't taken the opportunity of selling out.

They may have forgotten her long sentimental attachment to the place. She lived there for nearly 20 years after her late husband, Jack, took on the tenancy in 1952. And it was serving behind the busy bar that kept her going through the grim days when he took to heavy drinking and compulsive gambling. Born and brought up in London's East End, it was the noisy, cheerful atmosphere of the pub that helped Peggy cope with the otherwise low-key rural life she had married into. It became her home . . . and she nearly lost it twice.

At one point, Jack's behaviour got so bad the brewery threatened to sack him and Peggy ended up having to take on the licence herself. Later, when the brewery decided to sell up, it was Jack's Aunt Laura who came to the rescue. She helped them buy the freehold. That was in 1959 and it cost just £5600. Since then, a lot of money has been spent on the place but if she'd taken the offer, she would still have made a huge profit. Her family suspect the memory of her happier days with Jack means much more to her than the money.

Like so many rural pubs, The Bull has seen more than its fair share of village life. The rows and the romances, the gossip and the gripes of generations of Ambridge folk have unfolded before the landlords and barmaids of The Bull.

There's also been a fair amount of drama behind the bar! One of Peggy Archer's first barmaids was a young girl called Polly Mead, and

No bull . . . the regulars at Ambridge's favourite pub are delighted with the designer-noticeboard presented by one of their favourite magazines, Country Living. They don't even mind Mrs Snell abusing it for her own ends.

Happy bride, number one (right) . . . Ruth Pritchard joins the Ambridge dynasty as Mrs David Archer.

Happy bride, number two . . . Kathy Holland is delighted to register as the new Mrs Sid Perks.

history repeated itself when she later married Sid Perks and he was offered the tenancy by Mrs Archer. The licensing magistrates were deterred by Sid's record of juvenile delinquency and it was Polly who had to take over the licence.

Polly was killed in a car accident in 1982, leaving Sid to bring up his daughter, Lucy, on his own. He didn't find that altogether easy, nor does he today. Lucy has a Saturday job in a healthfood shop in Borchester and she has introduced disruptive ideas like alternative medicine to Ambridge (Sid's not ready for that!). He was remarried in 1987, to one of Lucy's teachers, Kathy Holland, but their household is still not without its tensions.

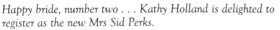

Lovely Lucy . . . growing up fast. Lucy Perks is showing too much independence for Sid's liking. He'd be happier if she settled for being a teenager a little while longer.

Another one-time barmaid at The Bull was Nora McAuley, an Irish girl who arrived in Ambridge expecting to marry Paddy Redmond, one of Dan Archer's hands at Brookfield Farm. Unknown to Nora, Paddy had been sowing a few wild oats with some of the local girls and her appearance put the cat among the pigeons. He quickly took flight and was later named as the father of Jennifer Archer's illegitimate child!

Nora got over the shock, stayed on and later became friends with George Barford, when he turned up as the new gamekeeper. She gave the village something to gossip about when she moved in with him and became pregnant. Sadly, she had a miscarriage and some time later she quietly left Ambridge. George Barford still lives here and is married to Christine Johnson (Phil Archer's sister), who runs the local stables.

In the intervening years, there have been a string of barmaids – some who delighted the regulars, others who dismayed them – but today, with Sid Perks trying to keep the peace between his daughter and his second wife, most of the drama seems to go on in the private quarters above the pub. He and Kathy seem none too happy. Kathy is out of sorts with her job as a teacher because she feels undervalued and underpaid. Sid would like her to work in The Bull full-time but that doesn't exactly appeal to her as a worthwhile career move. Cruel tongues hint at there being serious strains in the marriage.

With outsiders few and far between, the more sensitive regulars try to avoid personal matters and the bar-room gossip is, more often than not, about the new social and moral tensions in agriculture. Sid keeps the conversation well-fuelled with pints of Shires, while the Archers and their neighbours have fierce arguments about such contentious issues as genetic engineering, factory farming, hormones, pesticides, listeria, salmonella, set-asides, quotas and rural unemployment.

Next door to the pub is the village shop and post office and they say the gossip isn't nearly so good in there either since Martha Woodford

A landlord's work is never done . . . whenever anyone in Ambridge has anything to celebrate, it's invariably Sid Perks who has to pick up the empties.

retired and Betty Tucker took over. Martha's first husband was a postman and she worked all round the village doing everything from operating the petrol pumps at the garage to acting as daily help in several local houses. There wasn't much that went on that Martha didn't know about and after Joby (her second husband) died, in 1983, she had little more to interest her than recounting the snippets of conversation she'd overheard or was party to.

Betty Tucker is much more discreet. She and her husband, Mike, have had more than their fair share of woes, from bankruptcy to unemployment, and she's only too happy to keep things to herself. In any case, she's too busy trying to stock up with everything the villagers need . . . or even think they might need. She's been reading about the problems so many other small country stores have, competing with the spread of farm shops and the cheaper prices of the big town supermarkets, and she's very anxious not to do anything to make the owner, Jack Woolley, think about shutting down the Ambridge shop, leaving her once more without a job.

Again, it's not so obvious from Lakey Hill but the village main street does tell a story of changing times. The property just beyond Betty Tucker's shop used to be a thriving bakery but was converted into a house after its last owner retired in the late 1960s. Various owners had struggled to make a go of it for many years before that.

Going back to the 1950s, Ben White used to start work at two o'clock in the morning to have fresh bread and rolls on the shelves for the first farmworkers when they arrived at five o'clock. Doughy Hood bought it in 1963 but, within a couple of years, it was clear that he was having financial problems. He was bailed out by Mrs Laura Archer who went into partnership with him but that didn't last long and they sold out to a bigger company, Juniper Bakeries, who put in George Taylor to run it. It was when he left that it closed down altogether.

The house is now occupied by a Borchester businessman, Alexander Ralston, and his wife, Evelyn. Mr Ralston runs a small engineering company and his wife works part-time for British Rail, over at Hollerton Junction. They're a quiet, well-mannered couple who keep themselves very

Stone me . . . Bert Fry tried his hand at dry-stone walling but it soon became obvious that he was better at making up awful proverbs than building walls.

The wild and the woolly . . . Loveable though he was, Walter Gabriel never was much of a farmer and when (in the early 1970s) he owned a few fat lambs, he was heavily dependent on the advice of Dan Archer.

much to themselves, although they're always ready to support any of the village's activities.

Next door but one to The Bull is Woodbine Cottage, now the home of Bert Fry (who works over at Brookfield Farm for Phil Archer), his wife, Frieda, and a variable number of stray cats that he takes in from time to time. Bert's notoriety as folklorist with a story for every occasion was exploited by Elizabeth Archer, who works as a reporter for the *Borchester Echo*. He has even appeared on the regional television programme.

Opposite Woodbine Cottage is the police house, a fairly ugly pre-war brick building, now vacant, since Dave Barry was promoted from detective sergeant to inspector and moved back to Borchester.

Two doors away is the very busy doctor's surgery. The local GP is the young and unattached Dr Matthew Thorogood. He's a constant victim of idle gossip but the truth is, the only serious relationship he's had since coming to the village was with Caroline Bone, the manager of Grey Gables hotel and country club. Sadly that didn't work out and he tends to spend his lonely nights catching up on the latest medical publications that pour through his letterbox.

The village school is still one of Ambridge's most prominent buildings . . . except, of course, that it isn't a school any more. It was closed at the time of the great local government reorganisation in 1973. Today it's the village hall, scene of all the local community activities from the Women's Institute meetings to the Over-Sixties Club sessions. The old village hall (built in 1920 as a memorial to those who died in the Great War) was very badly damaged in 1976 by fire caused by an electrical fault and it proved too costly to repair. It was pulled down a few years ago and on the site, just beyond the duck pond and screened from the road by an evergreen hedge, lies Manorfield Close, a development of specially designed retirement bungalows.

The queen bee of the old folk who live there is Mrs Polly Perkins, mother of Peggy Archer and known to everyone as Mrs P. She's in number two and sees herself as the guardian of what's right and proper. Her next-door neighbour is the redoubtable Mrs Hannah Bagshaw, the only one able to hold her own with Mrs P.

Next to Manorfield Close there's an old black and white, thatched building with a delightful typically English garden. It's Honeysuckle Cottage, for many years the home of one of Ambridge's best-loved characters, Walter Gabriel. When he died, his son, Nelson, decided to sell the cottage to help solve some of the financial problems he was having with his Borchester wine bar. However, it didn't reach its reserve price at auction and he took it off the market. Now he lives there with his daughter, Rosemary, a policewoman in Borchester.

To the north of the village green, and opposite the village hall, are the village's 12 semi-detached council houses, each with a good vegetable plot and flower garden. One of them is the home of Neil and Susan Carter and their two children, Emma and Christopher. Young Christopher had a slightly shaky start in life . . . he was born with a hare lip but that has now been corrected with an operation.

A few doors away are Susan's family, the Horrobins, whose general rowdiness doesn't endear them to the rest of their neighbours. The Carters did try to help out by putting up Susan's brother, Clive, and his girlfriend, Sharon, when she became pregnant but it was all too much and they have since moved in with the vicar.

At the Borchester end of the main street, you can just see the tops of the petrol pumps at Ambridge's garage, opposite the village pond. There was great drama at the garage last year when the proprietor, Alan Goode, switched both his pumps to unleaded petrol and left half the village with the problem of getting their engines converted or going elsewhere for their petrol. He did a little to redeem himself by offering to do the conversions at half-price.

Even without his petrol shock, Mr Goode has never been the most popular man in the village (except with young Clive Horrobin, who is desperately trying to get himself a job as a mechanic). Alan Goode used to run a garage in Felpersham and he thought coming to Ambridge was a good move towards his retirement. Once he realised that running a business in such a small place was very hard work, he seemed to take it out on his customers with minimum service and maximum surliness. He might not have noticed but most of the locals now try to get their petrol on Wednesdays and Thursdays, when his wife, Jane, mans the pumps. She is as pleasant and chatty as he is dour and taciturn.

In the early 1960s, the garage was run by Paul Johnson (Christine Barford's first husband) and the mechanic was one of Tom and Prue Forrest's foster sons, Peter Stevens. Paul Johnson was a restless soul and he left Ambridge – and his wife – to go to work in London. Later, he moved on to Germany, where he died in a road accident.

The garage was then taken on by Haydn Evans, a very popular Welshman who arrived in Ambridge from his native Carmarthen, intending to set up a farm. He only settled for running the garage after he had tried and failed to make a go of running Willow Farm. A combination of bad luck and a bad back proved too much and even a partnership with Tony

Archer didn't help. Tony Archer, however, did get a wife out of the deal. Pat Archer is Haydn Evans's niece. She and Tony met when she came to look after Haydn when he had a slipped disc.

About half a mile to the south-east of the village, the nearest thing to an eyesore is a mid-Victorian monstrosity, Ambridge Hall, which lies trapped between the river and a long, sweeping bend on the Lower Croxley road. Built in 1860 for the local doctor of the day, by a squire with more money than taste, its yellow bricks and green tiles have now mellowed a little. And the present owners, Lynda and Robert Snell, have repainted the woodwork and guttering in gentle autumn colours and renovated the attractive wooden shutters on the windows.

The Snells bought the house after the previous owner, Mrs Laura Archer, died and it was inherited by her niece in New Zealand. Mrs Snell was very taken by the mature willow trees and beech trees in the garden and by the lawns that sweep right down to the river. Mr Snell is said to have resignedly reached for his cheque book without daring to argue.

Look who's come to tea . . . It's Uncle Tom, popping in to Brookfield where the kettle is always on the boil. Elizabeth still finds his stories funny but Shula's heard them all before.

Aren't they cuddly? . . .
And Ruth and David think the lambs are too!

Vintage Archers . . . Phil and Jill enjoy their status as the new
heads of the Ambridge dynasty. They've worked hard to follow
on the work of Dan and Doris in building up Brookfield Farm
and are now justly proud of the affection they get from their
friends and neighbours.

There aren't too many of the locals ready to argue with her, either, and when she started the protest against the proposed feeder road, no one demurred when she appointed herself 'Press and Publicity Officer, Manager and Media Consultant' for the campaign. Everyone also heaved a great sigh of relief when the plan was scrapped and they no longer had to suffer regular ear-bashings from Mrs Snell!

The lower slopes of Lakey Hill are part of Brookfield Farm, which has been in the Archer family for five generations, but the farmhouse is about a mile to the south, on the other side of the river, in the centre of one of Ambridge's medieval open fields and just below Ten Elms rise. It's easily spotted, part mellow brick and part black-and-white timbered and, like so many other local properties, dating back to the seventeenth century.

Now owned and run by Philip Archer, one of the most respected local farmers, Brookfield is a mixed farm with cows, pigs (kept at the Hollowtree unit), sheep and corn. It was originally a smaller, tenanted holding until Phil's father, Dan Archer, bought it in the 1950s and acquired several other parcels of land. At 450 acres, it isn't the biggest farm in the area but its importance was recognised in 1989, when it was used as the model farm for Food and Farming Year. That probably only made poor

Roll on the bus pass . . . Phil Archer smiles weakly at Jill's reminder of his sixtieth birthday. With David breathing down his neck, he's not too keen on marking round-figure dates!

On again, off again . . . Elizabeth Archer was engaged to Nigel Pargetter but not for long. It was all off by the time most people heard about it.

Phil feel even more embarrassed when slurry leaked from the farm into the river, killing 2000 fish. His daughter, Elizabeth, a reporter on the *Borchester Echo*, made matters worse by writing an article on the pollution before she knew it was her father's fault.

Brookfield wasn't altogether the happiest home in Ambridge in 1989. On top of the slurry incident, the Archers got embroiled in a blazing family row which most outsiders saw coming months beforehand. It was about that all-too-common farming phenomenon . . . a son anxious to find a proper role in life and a father not ready to retire. Now in his thirties, David Archer has, for some years, shown signs of frustration at having to play second fiddle at Brookfield. It all came to a head after he got married and there was nowhere for him and Ruth to live. They had to share Brookfield not just with Phil and Jill, but also with David's brother, Kenton, and sister, Elizabeth. It was a recipe for disaster.

When David was offered a job at Home Farm, with a house included in the deal, he jumped at it and he and Ruth left the family home. For Jill Archer, in particular, it was very traumatic and young Elizabeth didn't help by getting engaged to Nigel Pargetter and then breaking it off. When Kenton bought an antique shop in Borchester and went to live in the flat above it, Jill was very unhappy.

Ironically, it's the physical scars in the green field next to the old farmhouse that provide evidence that the family's emotional scars are healing. David is back working with Phil and the builders are working on a new home for him and Ruth. Peace could break out at any moment.

There's a second Archers' farm about a mile beyond Brookfield, out on the road to Felpersham. Mercifully screened from view by Oak Wood, Bridge Farm is another undistinguished late-Victorian pile, where the tenants are Philip Archer's nephew, Tony Archer, and his wife, Pat. They live there with their three children, Helen, John and Thomas. At Pat's instigation, they began changing to organic methods in 1984 and now all 140 acres

Have hard hat, will travel . . . Mike Tucker is keen to take full advantage of his forestry course and says he'll tackle any kind of woodman's work, anywhere.

Dairy maid . . . Pat Archer raised a few amused eyebrows when she launched her organic yoghurt. Who's laughing now that the business is so successful?

are free from modern chemicals.

Although it started with Pat's emotional and political instincts, it has also turned out to make good business sense. Recent figures show that sales of organic food are likely to soar from the current £42 million a year to more than £1 billion a year by 1999. Tony Archer says he'll be happy with a very small share of that and Pat is delighted because it spikes many of the old arguments. Factory-farming and the latest pesticides and chemical fertilisers are no longer the only way to survive economically, she says.

To the east and only about half a mile from the top of Lakey Hill there's Willow Farm, started from scratch by Haydn Evans and his son, Gwyn, in 1972. Haydn planned to develop a 100-acre dairy farm that he could eventually hand over to his son. Gwyn, however, had other ideas. He had never been keen on farming and when he fell in love with young Angela Cooper, who once worked in

the village stores, he left Ambridge.

Haydn then took Tony Archer into partnership but his back problems made it impossible for him to continue farming and he eventually gave it up to buy the local garage. Tony Archer moved to Bridge Farm and Mike Tucker, then the dairy manager at Brookfield (and secretary of the Farm Workers' Union), took on the tenancy of Willow Farm. That was in 1978.

The Tuckers – Mike and his wife, Betty – put a lot of hard work into the farm and might have made a real go of it if it hadn't been sold under them. Things didn't work out half as well when they moved to Ambridge Farm and Mike was forced into bankruptcy. Although most people think he should give up the idea, Mike still hopes to return to Willow Farm one day and he has therefore been obstructive to the present owner, Dr Matthew Thorogood, and his plans for possible barn conversions.

The Aldridge collection . . . Home Farm hasn't been the same since the arrival of Jennifer and Brian Aldridge's baby in 1988.

A close shave . . . Not for one of the Home Farm sheep (Brian wouldn't let Jennifer near them) but for a poor unsuspecting beast being used to prove she's a farmer's wife at heart during a visit to the Royal Show.

Just beyond Willow Farm, on the far side of the river, in front of Leaders Wood, there's a pair of estate cottages built in the mid-sixties by the late squire, Ralph Bellamy. One of them, Keeper's Cottage, is occupied by Prue and Tom Forrest. Tom, the late Doris Archer's brother, was the local gamekeeper for as long as anyone can remember and, even now when he's staring 80 in the face, he's only semi-retired. The other one, April Cottage, is home to Martha Woodford . . . when she's not putting upon poor Mrs Antrobus at Nightingale Farm!

At the southern edge of the wood, built on the foundations of the ancient Lyttleton Manor, is Home Farm, an early eighteenth-century building that was once divided into luxury flats. It was converted back into a farmhouse by Brian Aldridge, who bought 1500 acres of prime farmland from the Bellamy estate in 1975. Brian came to Ambridge from the Home Counties after his parents died in a car accident and the family farm was sold for building development. He married one of the Archer girls, Jennifer, who, a few years previously, had divorced her first husband, Roger Travers-Macy.

It's mainly her influence that can be seen in the rose garden, swimming pool and elaborate barbecue patio that make it look more like a country manor than a working farmhouse. A small block of holiday homes – glorying in the name, 'The Rookeries' – that Jennifer runs for pin money also adds to the non-agricultural appearance of Home Farm. It's easy to imagine that if Mrs Aldridge had her way the house might become Lyttleton Manor again.

Brian Aldridge is still recovering from a nasty accident that caused head injuries, two operations, a brain abscess, prolonged stays in hospital and then post-traumatic epilepsy. Through all this, they've had to call in help from Mike Tucker and David Archer, and Jennifer has found it increasingly difficult to cope with her 18-month-old baby, Alice, and 12-year-old Kate, who has been playing up recently. Her two other children, Adam and Deborah, live away from home. Adam works in London and Deborah is in her first year at Exeter University. If there wasn't this real angst in her life, Jennifer Aldridge would more than likely create it (she thrives on drama). She has also been trying to persuade Brian to try homoeopathy as a cure for his epilepsy. He is not amused.

Sweeping along the skyline back towards the village, on the other side of the bridge, you can see the Glebelands housing estate, a small, well-laid-out development of eight modern houses. They were built in the late seventies after Jack Woolley had acquired the land from the Bellamy Estate. Each of the eight houses is in the 'executive style' with four bedrooms, two bathrooms and its own patio. It's significant, perhaps, that most of the people who live there are newcomers and, with the exception of Derek Fletcher, who is a member of the parish council, they don't seem to get much involved in village life. But that didn't stop Kenton Archer offering to buy items for his antique shop from them and he appears to have done quite well out of it.

Opposite Glebelands, next to the church, is Glebe Cottage, a small, two-bedroomed brick house built around 1840. It's distinguished by a beautiful glass conservatory, added in 1970, and a lovely English cottage garden. It came into the Archer family when the lease was left to Doris Archer by the former squire's wife for whom she'd worked as a lady's maid. She was later able to buy the freehold and she and her husband, Dan, used it as their retirement home when they left Brookfield.

When Mrs Archer died, she left it to her granddaughter, Shula. She and her solicitor husband, Mark Hebden, moved in after her grandfather also died. Mark is in practice in Birmingham and Shula is a junior partner in Rodway and Watson, the company that manages the Bellamy estate. They have been trying to start a family for some time but without any luck so far. In 1989, they invested money in Shula's brother's move into the antique business and now they're keeping a close watch on how he's getting on.

Beyond Glebe Cottage and the church, there's Ambridge Farm, a 150-acre dairy holding run for many years by Ken and Mary Pound. They were very successful in rearing Friesian and Jersey cattle but came unstuck when they tried to cross-breed the two in the hope of producing a high-quality milk. When Ken died, the tenancy was taken over by Mike and Betty Tucker, who'd had to leave Willow Farm. They ran a milk-round and opened a farm shop but sadly the whole lot collapsed and Mike Tucker went bust in the winter of 1985. The land reverted to the Bellamy Estate and the new GP, Dr Matthew Thorogood, acquired a lease on the farmhouse, where he now lives.

Further west, snuggling in the bend of the river, is the very dilapidated Grange Farm. The farmhouse was built on eighteenth-century foundations and it looks as if there's been very little work done on it since. It's a mixture of stone, crumbling brick and cement rendering that's cracked and stained. Large pieces have already fallen away from the front wall and lie amid the other debris that surrounds the house.

The guilty tenants of the farm and its 150 acres are the Grundys. Joe Grundy, a widower, has long had a chip on his shoulder ever since his money-

Comic relief . . . Even the notorious Grundys joined in the fun of Red Nose Day but no one is quite sure if Clarrie ever did get the promised donation out of Joe and Eddie or if she just took it out of the housekeeping money.

making ventures in the seventies enraged most of the village. He staged a noisy autocross meeting and then an even noisier pop festival on his land. Neither made money and both cost him the few friends he had. He and his son, Eddie, survive because Eddie had the good sense to marry Clarrie Larkin. Simple soul that she may be, Clarrie has knocked the two men into something like farmers and when she's not trying to cope with her two young sons, William and Edward, she's working at making a garden out of the rubbish tip.

Farming doesn't come naturally to either Joe or Eddie and they're both constantly on the lookout for other ways of earning a crust. Eddie fancies

himself as something of a country and western singer and has got as far as cutting a couple of records. So far, however, he is still without fame and fortune. Joe, seeing himself as an entrepreneur, played around with acid house parties but, thankfully, that idea was as successful as everything else he touches . . . and the villagers were able to sleep on undisturbed by thousands of pop fans.

To the north-west, out on the Borchester road, a good mile's walk from the village centre you can just make out Blossom Hill Cottage, the home of another of the Archer family, Mrs Peggy Archer (sister-in-law of Philip Archer and mother of Lilian Bellamy – who has put the village in turmoil with her decision to sell the Estate – Jennifer Aldridge and Tony Archer). It's quite a small cottage, with just two bedrooms, but it has a pleasant sitting room with French windows leading out into the garden and, as an estate agent might say, it benefits from being adjacent to a country park and golf course. The gossips hint that Mrs Archer likes to be well out of the village so that no one can see the comings and goings of her friend, Godfrey Wendover.

One of the most popular places with the village children is Christine Barford's stables and riding school. Set within the country park, but run completely independently, Mrs Barford's thriving business is run from a rather nondescript brick-built house, with the stables and the indoor riding school built on at the back. It's actually very handy for her husband, George, because he's the local gamekeeper. George had hoped his son, Terry, might have followed in his footsteps when he was given the opportunity of training at Brian Aldridge's Home Farm. But, sadly, it didn't work out because Terry found it so difficult to settle back into civilian life.

For Christine Barford, this is the second time she has been involved in running the local stables. She was once in partnership with Grace Fairbrother (who was killed in a tragic fire), when they were both in their early twenties. However, later on, her

Poachers beware . . . gamekeeper George Barford can hear a twig crack at 100 yards and he doesn't take kindly to anyone interfering with his precious birds.

A stirring moment . . . but it didn't last. Jean-Paul thought he'd found a recipe for romance but Caroline Bone was more interested in his culinary craftsmanship than his amorous aspirations.

Boning up on his wine . . . The connoisseur Jack Woolley isn't too proud to seek a second opinion from Caroline Bone during a tasting session at Grey Gables. Even he doesn't realise it was Caroline who created the extensive wine list that attracts so much favourable comment from customers of the restaurant.

first husband, Paul Johnson, wasn't very keen on her riding and under pressure from him she sold out. Then she gave up riding altogether after a bad fall in which she broke two ribs and her collarbone.

It was while Paul was away on long business trips that she went back to help out her niece, Lilian, who had been running a riding school for several years. She's been there ever since and now nothing would part her from her beloved horses. She is totally dedicated and for more than ten years she has kept every Wednesday free for disabled children's sessions, which bring in young riders

from miles around. They have a wonderful time riding through the country park.

That country park and golf course are part of Grey Gables, headquarters of Jack Woolley's ever-growing empire. It's a late-Victorian gothic mansion set in magnificent parkland noted for its chestnut trees. Mr Woolley, a former Birmingham businessman, acquired it in 1962 and since then he's stocked the park with deer, developed an excellent shoot, built a golf course, added a swimming pool and established Grey Gables as a luxury hotel and restaurant.

Fancy seeing you here . . . Nelson Gabriel and Caroline Bone were having a gentle browse around Borchester's antique shops when who should turn up but the ubiquitous Detective Sergeant Barry. Nelson is guiltless for once, but Caroline isn't too sure!

In other circumstances, Mr Woolley, who also owns the *Borchester Echo*, might see himself as the squire. He certainly has a strong sense of duty to the community and he is always generous with his time and money. In fact he's becoming quite a philanthropist in his old age. His most recent venture was the creation of a new cricket pitch for the village team and he has given land to the local housing association to help build low-cost homes for local people.

Though some may see him as something of a name-dropper, Mr Woolley enjoys his moments of notoriety with an endearingly naive charm. He still talks about the visit he once had from Princess Margaret and the Duke of Westminster and it will be many moons before the locals are allowed to forget that his contribution to the 1989 Ambridge Spring Festival was a celebrity golf tournament that brought Terry Wogan to the village.

He has learned to take life a little easier these days and has become more and more reliant on the beautiful Caroline Bone to look after the general management of Grey Gables. Sometimes, however, his well-intentioned schemes tend to cause problems. In 1989, for instance, he arranged a murder mystery weekend without letting Caroline or the chef, Jean-Paul, know. They were not amused when the hotel was turned upside down by guests hunting for clues.

Another couple who are slowing down a little

are the Tregorrans, who live at Manor Court, on the other side of the country park, nearer the Borchester road. John and Carol Tregorran bought the fine eighteenth-century gentleman's house, set in 3 acres, as a showplace for John's antiques business as well as a home. Carol also created a vineyard and a large market garden. They have been among the village's most successful and popular couples but they are now both in semi-retirement and spend much of their time walking and quietly reading from the very extensive library that is John's pride and joy. John does the occasional bit of lecturing and he still has the antiques bug; every now and then he persuades Carol to join him on a round of the country house sales.

Once an arts centre run by John Tregorran's cousin, Hugo Barnaby, and later a youth club headquarters, Nightingale Farm has long since been converted into flats and it is now the place Mrs Marjorie Antrobus and her dogs call home. The farm has a useful range of outbuildings and 4 acres of garden and paddock (the rest was sold off long ago), and when Mrs Antrobus bought it, she converted the outhouses into kennels.

Mrs Antrobus is a classic example of what happens to people when they come to live in Ambridge. She first turned up in 1985 at the Over-Sixties Club to give a talk about breeding Afghan hounds. She happened to notice that Nightingale was for sale, fell in love with it, bought it and made it – and Ambridge – her home. Since then she has become part of the community. The villagers didn't take long to see beyond the gruff bossiness that hid her natural shyness and she's been able to shelter almost as many stray souls as stray dogs. Nigel Pargetter, Colonel Danby, Ruth Archer and Martha Woodford have all been grateful for her hospitality at some time in the past few years.

Every village needs a Mrs Antrobus. As a newcomer, the villagers sometimes find her a useful target to represent the big, bad outsider; at other times, they can show the generous spirit of the countryside . . . that makes even strangers feel at home in a place like Ambridge.

— CHAPTER THREE —
THE ACTORS AND THEIR CHARACTERS

WHEREVER A CHARACTER ORIGINATES, whether from the pen of a writer or the fertile imagination of the editor, the listener only makes contact with him or her through the actors and actresses. It's the members of the cast – the front-line troops – who people Ambridge and make it such a real community for so many of those who tune in every day.

When we recently advertised for a new editor we said we were looking for someone who thought actors were the most sensitive people on earth. It was an important requirement because they are sensitive souls and their sensitivity is reflected in the performances so crucial to the listeners' enjoyment of the programme.

There have been hundreds of them over the years . . . each adding their magic touch . . . the gravelly voice of Walter Gabriel; the measured silkiness of his son, Nelson; the corncrake of Mrs P.; the eternal cheerfulness of Jill Archer; the Yorkshire bluffness of George Barford; the sense of fun of Elizabeth Archer; or the awfulness of Eddie Grundy. By the raising of an eyebrow (which really does work on radio), putting a smile into the voice, finding a special way of saying 'Morning all', or using one of a thousand tricks of the trade, the players have breathed life into the lines.

At one time, some of the parts were typecast, and more importance was placed on a specific natural accent than on technical ability. Today, it's different. When the new editor auditions prospective

new members of the cast, what she's looking for is professionalism.

The programme is lucky enough to have two of the original cast still appearing regularly, lending their astonishing experience to newer members. June Spencer (who plays Peggy Archer) and Norman Painting (who plays Phil) were both in episode one, heard by the listening world on 1 January 1951.

June Spencer, now silver-haired and with a sense of humour undimmed by the trials and tribulations she's been through as Peggy Archer, is the ultimate professional. Despite all her years of creating the character for the microphone, she very positively leaves her at the studio door when she goes home, and she has never allowed the line between fact and fiction to blur.

June was born and brought up in Nottingham by very sensible parents who hated the idea of their daughter going on the stage. They wanted her to become a teacher and she exploited their ambition by taking music and drama lessons that could simply have led her to a career teaching little girls how to sing and speak nicely. Her parents were proud enough of her numerous school and amateur drama performances but what is not on record is how they coped with her later development . . . as an after-dinner entertainer doing the rounds of Masonic evenings, Rotary clubs, Women's Institutes, Townswomen's Guilds and the like with her early Joyce Grenfell monologues.

TRIAL   Norman family

"T H E   A R C H E R S"

Episode I — 1

Script by

EDWARD J. MASON   and   GEOFFREY WEBB.

Produced

by

GODFREY BASELEY.

O - 100

Cast:	Daniel Archer (the farmer)	Harry Oakes
	Doris Archer (his wife)	Nan Marriott Watson
	Philip Archer (younger son)	Norman Painting
	Christine Archer (daughter)	Pamela Mant.
	Jack Archer (elder son)	Denis Folwell
	Peggy Archer (his wife)	June Spencer
	Walter Gabriel (Dan's neighbour farmer)	Robert Mawdesley

1.   ANNOUNCER: Tonight Midland Region has pleasure in bringing

to the air its new farming family.......

THEME MUSIC

We present..... The Archers, of Wimberton Farm,

on the fringe of the village of Ambridge.

THEME MUSIC CONTINUES.

THEN FADES.

FADE IN ODD FARM NOISES.   COW MOOING (OFF MIKE!!)

FARM BACKGROUND.

2.   DAN.   Well Simon.   What d'you think?

3.   SIMON: Ah well - 'er might and 'er mightn't.

4.   DAN.   I know that - but what d'you think.

'It's true there weren't many other teenage girls on the circuit,' says June, 'but I thoroughly enjoyed myself and it was terrific experience learning how to work an audience.'

Her determination to overcome parental nervousness was strengthened when the BBC staged a talent competition in Nottingham and she entered, socked the panel with her version of Joan of Arc and won! She was given a spot in the winners' concert and the princely sum of 2 guineas. She was hooked.

Radio was then in its heyday and June quickly saw it as the road to fame and fortune. She became a radio actress and appeared in dozens of plays in Birmingham and London. One of them was a two-hander, *Time Wasted*, in which she starred opposite Denis Folwell. It was about an engaged couple spending a day in the countryside at the girl's insistence. The man spent most of the time complaining, and they ended up in a village pub with him enjoying the noisy, friendly atmosphere and her complaining.

If that reminds you of Peggy and Jack Archer, you could be right. Godfrey Baseley obviously saw it that way because, unknown to June, he decided to cast her and Denis in *The Archers*. June found out about his plan while she was standing in the canteen queue at the BBC studios in Birmingham.

'I was waiting for a cup of tea when another young actress, Pamela Mant, started talking to me about how she was going to play a girl called Christine Archer in this new series and she was looking forward to working with me. I was very surprised because no one had talked to me about it and, to be honest, I wasn't very interested. I was doing lots of lovely plays and, at the time, they were much more exciting for me.'

However, the offer of the part did come . . . with a very detailed briefing about the character. Peggy Archer was a working-class girl from the East End of London. Her father was a railway porter and he had wanted her to become a dressmaker. At the outbreak of war, she'd changed her mind and joined the Auxiliary Territorial Service (ATS, now WRAC) and that's how she met young Jack Archer, a country lad from Ambridge in Borsetshire. They had married and, in the first trial script,

she was facing an unplanned pregnancy.

June had been specialising in a wide range of dialects and was easily able to conceal her Midland accent behind the brittle cockney vowels. Godfrey Baseley, ever the perfectionist, abandoned the usual auditioning style and instead invited her in for an interview . . . in character and without a script. It was a tough test and two leading actresses (those hoping to play Doris Archer and Grace Fairbrother), who had been in the trial episodes, didn't get through.

At that stage, June wasn't over-excited. 'It was just another little job as far as I was concerned and there certainly wasn't any talk of it going on for a long time.'

Her experience earned her the top rate . . . £12 for five episodes a week . . . and she began to feel that it was no longer just 'another little job'. It needed a completely different technique from her other work. 'Godfrey was quite certain of what he wanted and he was determined to get it. He told us he didn't want any fancy histrionics. He wanted the listeners to be convinced that they were overhearing conversation between members of a real family and not a bunch of actors acting.'

Godfrey and the listeners clearly got what they wanted because the programme grew ever more popular; and June and her colleagues became stars who were fêted wherever they went. But June's feet were kept firmly on the ground by her businessman husband and her family. In the studio, she continued to consolidate the character of Peggy Archer and all went well until the early seventies. Then the programme itself went into the doldrums, but for June the problems were compounded by the death of Denis Folwell and subsequently, her stage husband, Jack. 'The script had the widowed Peggy moving out of The Bull to become manageress and live in at Grey Gables. It was a crazy move and Peggy would have been totally out of her depth.'

That's not how the writers played it, though. There were several changes in the team and they seemed to lose the essential elements of Peggy's personality somewhere along the way. The cockney girl slowly became an over-confident, bossy lady-of-the-manor type and June Spencer found herself working against the script for the first time.

'I was very upset. I felt I was losing faith with the listeners, that I was letting them down. The real Peggy was drifting further and further away. I kept reminding everyone that Peggy was Mrs P.'s daughter but no one took any notice! It got so bad that I seriously thought about giving it up. It was only because my husband kept telling me how much I'd miss it all that I kept going.'

June was eventually reconciled to the changes and these days she feels much happier about Peggy. 'She's got a good relationship with her mother and things are all right between her and Tony. She never sees Lilian, of course, but I think the tensions between her and Jennifer are quite natural.'

What about the romantic interest? How does she view the relationship with Godfrey Wendover, or Captain Pugwash, as Tony Archer calls him?

'Oh that's fun. I don't think collecting your bus pass should suggest you're past falling in love. I've got an elderly relative who got into trouble for having sex with a man in her room at the nursing home and I thought that was terrific. She's in her eighties and the man must have found her attractive enough to go to her room because even if her walking aid had been on wheels it would have taken all night for her to get to his!'

The laughter that accompanied the telling of that story underlines the one regret June has about the current Peggy. She doesn't have much of a sense of humour.

Norman Painting's involvement with *The Archers* goes back even before the first national broadcast. He played the young farmer, Philip Archer, in the pilot series made for the Midlands Home Service earlier in 1950 and has earned a place in the *Guinness Book of Records*, as the world's longest-running radio actor.

Beyond that, Norman has also written nearly 1200 scripts for the programme, under the pen name Bruno Milna, and it's understandable that he feels he has sunk much of his own identity into it. He happily accepts that his alter-ego probably has a much better-known name than his own.

Born in Leamington Spa on St George's Day in 1928, the son of a railway signalman, Norman Painting left grammar school at 15 because his father said he couldn't afford to keep him in full-time education any longer. Undeterred by this temporary setback, he spent three years working as a librarian and saved enough money to see himself through Birmingham University, a first-class degree in English and a research scholarship to Christ Church College, Oxford. 'Oxford just after the war was a good place for someone like me,' he says. 'I was dabbling in acting, directing and writing but I also had a growing interest in archaeology and Old English.'

He became a tutor in Anglo-Saxon at Exeter College, was elected President of the university Archaeological Society and joined the Oxford University Dramatic Society (OUDS) as an actor.

'Kenneth Tynan was producing *Hamlet* at the time and I remember his reaction when I couldn't accept his invitation to take a part in it because I had a previous engagement. He just cut me dead. Without saying a word, he fixed me with a fishy eye, tossed his head back and roared past me. It was a splendid performance.'

Two other members of OUDS at the time were Shirley Williams and Peter Parker (who later became the boss of British Rail), and Norman found that the lure of the greasepaint soon became stronger than his interest in academia. After two years, he abandoned his research and left Oxford for a career in broadcasting. 'I've never regretted the decision,' he says quite firmly.

That decision took him into the new and insecure world of the freelance, never certain from where the next crust would come, but it suited him. He enjoyed his independence and when he was offered a staff job with the BBC in Birmingham, he turned it down. Instead, he went on writing, researching, presenting programmes and acting, picking up fees wherever he could. That was in 1949 and since then he has written dozens of radio plays and documentaries and appeared in numerous radio and television programmes.

It was, of course, as Philip Archer that he made his name. Like June Spencer, he insists that there were few similarities between him and the fictional farmer's son. 'I did like him, though. He was a bit of a tearaway, a ram, double-dating, big-headed but with a heart as big as a bucket.' And taking on the role was a terrific challenge. 'It was like acquiring a

new identity. We had almost to become the person we were portraying.'

How well he rose to the challenge can be seen in the rewards. In 1976 he was awarded an OBE for services to broadcasting, and the Royal Agricultural Society of England made him its only life governor 'in recognition of his 25 years' service to agriculture'.

To coincide with the twenty-fifth anniversary of *The Archers*, he wrote his autobiography, *Forever Ambridge*, in which he told, for the first time from an actor's viewpoint, the story of how the programme began and how it developed over the years:

The characters and dialogue had a freshness and naturalness that was new: the atmosphere, the sound effects and the characters' reactions to farming matters were authentic. There was a liberal lacing of humour and the skill of the writers ensured that the end of each episode left listeners with such teasing and unanswered questions that they felt they had to listen to the next day's episode.

Forever Ambridge was a tremendous success and Norman updated and republished it with equal success for the thirtieth anniversary.

In 1982, however, Norman suffered a series of heart attacks, during which he was 'dead' for three minutes. Despite that, he still undertakes a huge range of public activities on top of his professional work. He is involved in the Hospice Movement; he preached a sermon in St Alban's Abbey at the start of European Year of the Environment; he took a major part in the inaugural service for the Church Urban Fund in Westminster Abbey; and he is a patron of the Tree Council.

In recent years he has continued his acting career in theatres all round the country, including his favourite to date, the Birmingham Rep, where he scored a personal success in David Storey's *The Contractor*.

Since Christ Church, his old Oxford college, made him a member of High Table, one of his chief delights is dining there.

Norman Painting (Phil Archer)
and June Spencer (Peggy Archer)

THE OTHER MEMBERS OF THE CAST

ROSALIND ADAMS (Clarrie Grundy) studied at the Royal College of Music before becoming an actress. She began her radio career as Tracey in Radio 2's *Waggoner's Walk*, in which she and Patricia Gallimore (Pat Archer) played flatmates.

Most of her work today is in radio but she has had a lot of fun in the theatre and television. Her favourite job was creating the part of Annie in *The Norman Conquests* at Alan Ayckbourn's Theatre-in-the-Round, Scarborough.

Rosalind is the daughter of one actress and the mother of another. Her 11-year-old daughter, Melissa, has already appeared in several radio plays. She loves plants and languages and would love to travel more. The world of Ambridge is definitely not big enough for her!

Rosalind Adams (Clarrie Grundy)

Bob Arnold
(Tom Forrest)

Sam Barriscale
(John Archer)

Yves Aubert
(Jean-Paul)

BOB ARNOLD (Tom Forrest) was born on Boxing Day, 1910, in the Cotswold village of Asthall, which lies in the Windrush Valley halfway between Minster Lovell and Burford. He left school at 14 to work for a butcher in Burford and was paid 5 shillings a week.

'My father kept The Three Horse Shoes village pub at Asthall, but sadly it didn't make enough profit to support us,' says Bob. When he was just 22, he was seriously ill and spent 15 months in hospital with a tubercular spine. 'When I came out of hospital the only job I could get was painting white lines on roads for Oxfordshire County Council.'

It was while growing up in the village pub that Bob heard the old men singing traditional Cotswold folk songs, and years later he remem-

bered the words and music and put them on record.

In 1937, Bob got his big chance in broadcasting. A programme called *In the Cotswolds* was being made, and as Bob was well-known round Burford as a singer and story-teller, he was invited to take part. That led to other BBC Midlands programmes, and he soon found himself being billed in variety shows as Bob Arnold, the Farmer's Boy.

After wartime service in the RAF, he returned to radio in *Children's Hour* and radio plays. When he first auditioned for *The Archers* in 1950, he was told he'd never be used on the programme because he had such a recognisable accent!

Of course, there was a change of heart and some four months later he was offered the part of Tom Forrest, the role he's been playing ever since.

For more than 30 years he introduced the Sunday omnibus with his famous 'Morning all.'

'Like Tom I'm getting on a bit,' says Bob, 'but I'm still happy playing the odd episode, and we both look forward to being around for a little while longer yet!'

YVES AUBERT (Jean-Paul) is a Frenchman of suitably romantic birth. His mother is Hungarian, and his father a Parisian actor. So it seemed natural for Yves to follow in his father's footsteps and one of his great wishes is to play opposite him.

He came to England to learn the language but liked it so much that he stayed, although the English way of life still surprises him. Some years ago, he was invited to lunch at a farm in Wiltshire. The bottle of wine he brought along was accepted with grace, then it was put on the sideboard and he was offered a cup of tea after the meal!

Besides voice-overs, his work in England has included fringe plays like *The Balcony* and *Swiss Cheese*, in which he played the parts of the General and Swiss Cheese respectively. His first work for BBC television was a six-part French language course, *Dès le Début*, but he has since appeared in programmes ranging from *Grange Hill* and the short serial *Diana*, to an episode of *Bergerac*. He has also appeared in the American mini-series remake of *Around the World in Eighty Days* and in *The Bill*, for Thames Television.

Good food is important to him, as it is to most Frenchmen, and playing Jean-Paul comes naturally. When he isn't acting, he enjoys entertaining friends and testing his expertise in the kitchen. Now, more than ever, his friends have high expectations of his culinary skills.

His other relaxation is the thoroughly English pastime of gardening, especially in his herb garden. He also loves walking with his sheepdog, Katz.

SAM BARRISCALE (John Archer) was born in September 1974, in Worcester, and has the perfect background for his role in *The Archers* . . . he lives on a farm on the outskirts of the city.

He first thought about becoming an actor when he saw his older brother, James, in *Rough Justice* at the local Swan Theatre, where he later took his first speaking role as one of the Cratchits in *A Christmas Carol*. From there he went on to do plays like *Under Milk Wood* and *A Servant of Two Masters*. Then he changed his mind and decided he wanted to work on the technical side of the theatre, joining the crew for productions like *Grease*, *Cabaret* and *Oliver Twist*.

In the summer of 1987, however, Sam was acting again, in Willy Russell's *Our Day Out*. And that was when a BBC producer from Pebble Mill visited Worcester to audition children for the parts of John and Helen Archer. Sam auditioned with a friend, Frances Graham, and they got the parts.

While he was appearing in *The Archers* Sam was noticed by Vanessa Whitburn (then the senior drama producer at Pebble Mill but now editor of Channel 4's *Brookside*) and he was cast in Philip Martin's *Pillars of Society* on Radio 4. From there, a Royal Shakespeare Company scout cast him in *The Rise of Edward IV*.

When Sam leaves school he wants to go to drama school to become a professional actor.

JUDY BENNETT (Shula Hebden) was educated at a Liverpool convent grammar school and gave her first public performance when she was 14 . . . playing St Bernadette at a festival in the city's Philharmonic Hall. After studying at the Guildhall School of Music and Drama, she got her first job as an assistant stage manager and understudy in *The Chinese Prime Minister* at the Globe Theatre, only to be sacked for not having an Equity card. She did a walk-on part in *Emergency Ward 10*, got her union card and returned to The Globe as assistant stage manager/understudy in *The Cavern*.

In 1966 she auditioned for BBC Schools Radio, and was cast as a boy by producer, Richard Wortley. More radio work rapidly followed, including parts in *The Dales* and *Waggoner's Walk*. In June 1971 she joined *The Archers* to play the young Shula and, because she specialises in children's voices, she also successfully played Shula's twin brother Kenton, sister Elizabeth, and then Adam Travers-Macy! Her voice is often heard (though not always recognised) on television, where she has brought to life characters in puppet series and cartoons like *Rupert the Bear*, *Mumfie*,

Judy Bennett (Shula Hebden) recording with Trevor Harrison (Eddie Grundy) in 1980.

Cloppa Castle, *The Munch Bunch* and *The Perishers*.

She also presented the pre-school radio programme, *Playtime*, for nine years, and has taken lead roles in many radio plays, including Pip in *Great Expectations* and David in *David Copperfield*.

Judy is married to Charles Collingwood (who plays Brian Aldridge) and has three children, Toby, Barnaby and Jane.

TIMOTHY BENTINCK (David Archer) is one of the few members of the cast with any practical experience of agriculture. He was born on a sheep station in Tasmania and worked on farms for pocket money throughout his childhood. 'My parents emigrated but came back to England for some conversation,' he says.

After university, Tim took time off to help his father and stepmother renovate and stock a small-holding in Devon. He has also delivered twin lambs in a snowstorm on New Year's Eve and hand-milked a cow every morning for a year.

'I find some of David Archer's sneering lines about organic farming stick in my throat, not to mention his mockery of long-haired, Green liberals who work in television, since that's pretty much what I am,' he admits.

Born in 1953, Tim was educated at Harrow, the University of East Anglia and the Bristol Old Vic Theatre School, where he won the Carlton Hobbs radio drama competition and joined the BBC Radio Rep for six months. He has recorded more than 100 radio plays and has also worked extensively in films and television. His theatre appearances are supplemented by lots of voice-overs, dubbing, language tapes and TV ads.

The high point of his career was playing the dashing Pirate King in the jazzed up *Pirates of Penzance* at Drury Lane. He is perhaps best known for playing the cavalier hero Tom Lacey in the BBC serial, *By The Sword Divided*, and the appalling Nigel Barrington in LWT's sitcom, *Square Deal*.

When he isn't acting, he writes and records music. And in 1989 he invented The Hippo, a child-carrying device, featured in the *Sunday Times* Innovation Awards.

He lives in a Victorian house in London and is slowly renovating it with his wife, Judy, and two sons, William and Jasper.

GRAHAM BLOCKEY (Robert Snell) was born in Manchester and brought up in Scotland by his medical parents (his father is a retired orthopaedic surgeon). He went to boarding school in Edinburgh for four unhappy years; then, before going to Newcastle University to study medicine, he had much more fun working as a housefather in a home for physically handicapped children. During his medical studies he spent three months doing circumcisions in a mission hospital in rural Kenya!

After becoming a houseman and doing his stint in medicine and surgery at Shottery Bridge Hospital, Durham, and working in casualty at St Mary's, Paddington, he traded in his stethoscope to join Bristol Old Vic Theatre School. He was there for a year, during which he worked as a medical locum in the holidays. He then spent three years in

Timothy Bentinck (David Archer)

Graham Blockey (Robert Snell)

touring theatre in the West Country and in the Lake District.

When the bills got too high and the theatre money too low, Graham went back to medicine to make ends meet and that allowed him to do some fringe theatre in London before joining the BBC Radio Rep. Ironically, he auditioned unsuccessfully for the role of Dr Thorogood before joining *The Archers*, in 1986, as Lynda Snell's computer expert husband.

'Since then,' he says, 'I've done bits and pieces of telly, bits and pieces of medicine, mainly casualty locums in local hospitals, some lovely parts in some excellent radio plays and some not so good ones, and I have produced several occasional quiz programmes for a medical television company. I've done a few telly adverts – the *Financial Times* scientist, the Hi-Tec marathon runner, Greenall's bitter drinker and Mitchell's Car Hire wally.'

Graham is married to Chris Ingram, a writer and journalist, and lives in Farnham. He has two children, Olivia and Jamie.

He ran in the London marathon for the first time in 1989 and was sponsored by the cast and production team.

CAROLE BOYD (Lynda Snell) was born and brought up in London and always considered herself a townie until arriving in Ambridge in 1986. Since then, she has acquired a garden on an island in the Thames and, in true Lynda Snell style, has pestered the expert gardeners in the cast as to what to grow in it.

Word of this somewhat obsessive behaviour got around and she was invited on to *The Gardening Quiz* (perhaps as an attempted cure). Unfortunately the experience, though most enjoyable, did nothing to help her battle against greenfly.

Carole is no stranger to radio soaps; she played Shirley Edwards in Radio 2's *Waggoner's Walk* for four years and can be heard regularly in radio drama

Carole Boyd (Lynda Snell) and friend Persephoue

Margot Boyd (Mrs Antrobus)

and features productions. She records books-on-cassette for various publishers and was co-presenter on the enormously successful series for children, *Little Storyteller*. She is also the voice behind many radio and television commercials.

Her work in theatre spans some 20 years, including a year working with Alan Ayckbourn in Scarborough, where she created the role of June in *Way Upstream*. She has also appeared in an episode of BBC 1's *Campion*, in which she hopes she was unrecognisable as the awful Mrs Pole.

MARGOT BOYD (Mrs Antrobus) had, while studying at the Royal Academy of Dramatic Art, the rare distinction of taking part in a play (*Heartbreak House*) produced by George Bernard Shaw. And that was only the start of a glittering theatrical career that has included many West End productions. 'I was particularly lucky to play opposite A. E. Matthews, my favourite actor, in comedy, in *The Manor at Northstead*,' she says.

In 1953, she had a season at Stratford and it was then that she also made her first radio broadcast from the BBC's Birmingham studios. After that came the musical *Divorce Me, Darling* and the play she has enjoyed acting in most of all, *Waiting in the Wings* by Noel Coward.

Her television work has included *Dixon of Dock Green*, and she was invited to join the BBC Drama Repertory Company in 1969. 'Since then radio has been my first love,' says Margot. It was while working on the Radio Rep in London that she was given a small one-off part in *The Archers* and made such a success of it that she was written into the programme as a regular character.

NIGEL CARRINGTON (Nigel Pargetter) is always at a loss when it comes to biographies because he doesn't feel he has any specific roots. His father's military career took the three-year-old Nigel away from his native Warwickshire to the four corners of England and to such diverse places

Nigel Carrington (Nigel Pargetter)

Charles Collingwood (Brian Aldridge)

as Germany and Singapore. Arriving home and having completed his education in North Yorkshire, he was accepted by the Guildhall School of Music and Drama in London.

A tour with the Prospect Theatre Company began his professional career in 1977, then there were three years of living out of a suitcase in rep. Various television roles were followed by excursions into soap as Greg (Heather's assistant) in *Brookside*, and parts in *The Practice, Coronation Street, Emmerdale Farm* and *Albion Market*.

Nigel now lives in Cheshire with his wife, Susan, and is constantly rushing here and there recording voice-overs for every conceivable purpose and appearing in video productions for large businesses.

He is an avid reader and he likes to keep in trim by cycling, swimming and running. His main ambition, like every actor, is to keep working. But he also wants to travel the world and find a cure for hayfever!

CHARLES COLLINGWOOD (Brian Aldridge) was born in Canada in 1943 but the family came back to England the following year and he grew up in the country, near Andover. He went to Sherborne School, where he shocked his housemaster by saying he wanted to be a nightclub pianist.

He did go to the Royal Academy of Dramatic Art, however, and embarked on a career as an actor. 'It took me six years to earn enough to pay tax,' he recalls. 'I did various ghastly jobs, like cleaning and delivering boxes of fruit and vegetables round Marble Arch.'

By 1973, he had worked with several repertory companies and was playing in *How The Other Half Loves* with Penelope Keith at Greenwich. Shortly after that, he met actress Judy Bennett, who was playing Shula in *The Archers*, and they recorded three children's puppet series together for ATV – *Mumfie, Cloppa Castle* and *The Munch Bunch*. 'After 150 shows together, we realised we were meant for each other and got married.'

When he's not working, Charles is a passionate club cricketer (mostly with the Stage Cricket Club) and a very keen gardener. He and Judy live in London, and their daughter, Jane, was born in 1979, when Charles was playing in *Dirty Linen* at the Arts Theatre as well as *The Archers* – which made it a very busy year!

Charles has had a varied career, one minute co-hosting a television quiz series with Bernard Manning, the next reading the news on the BBC World Service, and then back to performing in Richard Stilgoe's highly successful radio shows.

His television appearances include *The Bretts*, *Hot Metal*, *Hannay*, *Inspector Morse* and an episode of *King and Castle*, in which he played the part of a pseudo old Etonian secondhand car salesman. 'Was that typecasting?' he asks himself . . .

SARA COWARD (Caroline Bone) has, in real life, absolutely no connection with the English aristocracy. In fact, she is a grammar-school girl from south-east London, who went on to train at Bristol University's drama department. After gaining an honours degree in English and Drama, she returned to London and the Guildhall School, where she won the Carlton Hobbs award for radio drama. That gave her an Equity card and a six-month contract with the BBC Drama Repertory Company and she has enjoyed doing radio work ever since.

She also works in television, does occasional films and acts in a wide selection of provincial and London theatres. She has co-written plays for the London fringe and has the distinction of having a chapter to herself in Clive Swift's book, *The Performing World of the Actor*.

Whenever Caroline disappears on a skiing trip or to a Greek island, it's because Sara is performing on a stage or in a television studio somewhere in the country. So far, she has always found her way back to Ambridge after these excursions. For the future . . . who knows?

PAMELA CRAIG (Betty Tucker) first appeared on the professional stage as Peter Pan at the Theatre Royal, Leicester, when she was 15. After that she went to the Birmingham Theatre School, where Alan Devereux was a fellow pupil. She has worked extensively in rep (including a stint with the Traverse Theatre in Edinburgh), and spent several years working in radio drama in Manchester and Leeds, doing plays by Alan Plater, Henry Livings, Trevor Griffiths and Alan Ayckbourn. She also worked with Alfred Bradley and Alan Ayckbourn in Leeds on a version of D. H. Lawrence's *Daughter-in-law*, in which she played the title role.

In the West End, Pamela was directed by John Osborne in Charles Wood's *Meals on Wheels*. Her television appearances include episodes of *Z Cars*; 13 weeks in *Coronation Street* (as Jackie Marsh, a journalist who had an affair with Ken Barlow); *The Pickersgill Primitive* by Mike Stott; the matron in BBC's *Horizon* programme, *Joey*; and the wife in *William Blake* (BBC). She also enjoys working in fringe theatre.

In her private life, Pamela is married to actor Terence Brook, who is still recognised (despite beard and spectacles) as the 'lonely man' of Strand cigarette adverts in the 1960s!

Sara Coward (Caroline Bone)

*Pamela Craig
(Betty Tucker)*

*Michael Deacon (Reverend
Jerry Buckle)*

MICHAEL DEACON (Reverend Jerry Buckle) was born in Scotland and he spent the first five years of his career in theatres all over the country. In Edinburgh, Tyrone Guthrie saw him working and cast him in his production of *The Three Estates*.

He has appeared at Birmingham Repertory Theatre and in *The Hippolytus* at the Hampstead Theatre Club. This was followed by a season at the Bristol Old Vic with roles in *The Cherry Orchard*, *Lock Up Your Daughters* and *The Merchant of Venice*.

His television appearances include Haemon in *The Antigone* (BBC 2); Firebrace in *A King and His Keeper* (BBC 2); Chris Lazenby in *The Black Room* (a Paul Temple thriller on BBC 1); *Callan*; and *New Scotland Yard*. He also played Les Rawley in John Schlesinger's film, *A Kind of Loving*, and was seen at the 1973 London Film Festival, playing the lead in *Matushka*, directed by John Lind.

His radio roles include Brother Martin to Joan Plowright's *Saint Joan*, and the lead in a serialisation of Stendhal's *The Charterhouse of Parma*, opposite Geraldine McEwan. During an 18-month contract with the BBC Radio Drama Company, he took leading roles in some very diverse plays: an adaptation of Plato's *Symposium*, Shakespeare's *Taming of the Shrew*, Saki's *A Watched Pot*, several light entertainment programmes and new drama of all descriptions.

In 1989, he played Creon in a successful production of *Medea* at the Gate Theatre, Notting Hill, and Jamie in *Long Day's Journey into Night* at the Arts Theatre and Westminster Theatre.

Michael has lectured for the University of Arkansas in America, and his hobbies include natural history ('If King Lear was on one channel and a natural history programme on the other, King Lear would have to wait!'), and gardening. (He uses containers on the balcony of his London maisonette, which he shares with his three cats, and once produced 26 pounds of tomatoes!) He also listens to music and reads a lot.

He is an enthusiastic supporter of the Greens and says the pollution of the environment fills him with rage.

Alison Dowling
(Elizabeth Archer)

Richard Derrington
(Mark Hebden)

Alan Devereux (Sid Perks)

RICHARD DERRINGTON (Mark Hebden) started his career in repertory at Birmingham and then with Alan Ayckbourn's company in Scarborough. He followed this with seasons at Salisbury, Liverpool, St Andrews and Nairobi, before joining the Royal Shakespeare Company for three years to play in a major cycle of history plays directed by Terry Hands. This included two international tours in *Henry V* and *Coriolanus*, as well as the role of Alan in *The Dance of Death* at the Aldwych, and *Awful Knawful* at the Warehouse.

He then toured the world with the Old Vic Company in Derek Jacobi's *Hamlet*. And his other theatre work includes Puck in *A Midsummer Night's Dream*, Sydney in *Absurd Person Singular* (at Leatherhead), and William of Orange in *Glorious Years* (at Theatre Clwyd).

Richard has appeared on television in *Pericles*, as Sordido in *Women Beware Women*, and as Alan in *Marjorie and the Preacher Man*. On radio he has played many of the classic roles: Puck, Feste, Osvald in *Ghosts*, and Jacques in *Jacques and His Master* (with Alan Bennett).

Taylor's Tickler, the one-man play written specially for him by Anthony Naylor, has now been seen at venues all over England, ranging from private drawing rooms to the National Theatre. In the USA it has toured from Las Vegas to Oklahoma City and Santa Fe. It has also been recorded by the BBC World Service as their *Play of the Week*.

He has now added to his repertoire, *The Last Plantagenet*, a new play about a close relative of Richard III (first performed in 1987), and *The Campden Wonder*, a two-hander which he performs with Roger Hume, who plays Ambridge's Bert Fry.

Richard lives with his wife, Louise, and son,

Giles, in a renovated cottage deep in the Gloucestershire countryside, surrounded by ducks and chickens . . . and the children who attend the nursery school his wife runs.

ALAN DEVEREUX (Sid Perks) was born in 1941 and went to school in Sutton Coldfield. When he was 14, he started going to evening classes to study speech and drama, and a year later he went to the Birmingham Theatre School. BBC radio plays soon followed and he had several walk-on parts in television. He made his first professional stage appearance at Birmingham Repertory Theatre in 1956.

'I spent five years in stage management with Derek Salberg's repertory companies at the Alex Theatre in Birmingham and the Grand in Wolverhampton,' he recalls. 'Working as an assistant stage manager in weekly rep, and playing small parts, is a very thorough way to learn about the theatre.'

Alan has played the part of Sid Perks since 1962, and is half of the only father/daughter partnership on the programme. His daughter, Tracy-Jane White, plays clever, grammar-school girl, Lucy Perks. He has also performed in over 100 radio plays, supplied voice-overs for countless audio-visual films for industry, appeared in three tv ads and voiced thousands of radio commercials.

Alan still lives in Sutton Coldfield, and has been married since 1966. As well as daughter Tracy-Jane, who is now married and living in London, he has a son called Ross.

ALISON DOWLING (Elizabeth Archer) spent Christmas 1988 working alongside Phil Archer and Eddie Grundy, would you believe? In the guise of a good-but-naughty fairy, she performed with Norman Painting and Trevor Harrison in pantomime at the Horsham Arts Centre.

'Elizabeth's frequent absences from the programme have been written in not only for her to hunt hunks on Bondi Beach but to enable me to present the Saturday morning children's television show, *TX*, for Granada,' says Alison. She enjoyed working alongside Derek Jacobi in the film *Little Dorrit* but, she recalls: 'The corset was agony!'

When former editor, William Smethurst, left to become boss of Central Television's *Crossroads*,

Alison enjoyed playing the part of Lisa Lancaster. After that, in 1988, she joined the London Shakespeare Group (LSG) and toured the Middle East, starting in the United Arab Emirates and going on to Oman, Iraq and Egypt. In the autumn of 1988, she toured Canada, playing Hero in *Much Ado About Nothing* and her last performance with the LSG was in Bangkok.

FELICITY FINCH (Ruth Archer) says her first professional job was a real baptism of fire, working backstage on a national tour of *The King and I*. She remembers many an all-nighter, altering 20 costumes to fit each new group of Siamese children and being so tired that the chorus's dresses were sewn back to front!

After eight months as an assistant stage manager, she spent three years training at the Drama Centre and then went on to work in repertory in Leeds, Leicester, Nottingham, Northampton, Newcastle and Cardiff; and in Hong Kong, Australia and Europe, with the Old Vic Company.

Felicity Finch (Ruth Archer)
relaxes with 'husband' Timothy Bentinck (David Archer).

Felicity has played a great variety of parts, from Jessica in *The Merchant of Venice* to Violet Beauregarde in *Charlie and the Chocolate Factory*. Her favourites have been a Spanish-Geordie 'lady of the night' ('You don't come across that accent every day!') in Tom Hadaway's *The Long Line* for Live Theatre in Newcastle, and Laura in *The Glass Menagerie* in Cardiff. Her television work has included *Angels*, *No Place Like Home* and the BBC serialisation of *Bleak House*, in which she played Rosa.

Felicity comes from Teesside, where her family still live. The love of her life is a director and writer in Cardiff, she has a base in London and *The Archers* is produced in Birmingham, so much of her life is spent at the mercy of British Rail. The part of Ruth, and her growing involvement in Ambridge, has been a completely new experience for Felicity. She had never previously done any radio work and no one was more surprised when David and Ruth's relationship really took off. She was genuinely shocked when she read the script instruction, 'David kisses Ruth.' Since then, combines and pigs have taken on a whole new meaning in her life!

PATRICIA GALLIMORE (Pat Archer) began her acting career by winning the BBC Radio Drama Competition (now known as the Carlton Hobbs Award), and from drama school in Birmingham went to the BBC Radio Drama Company in London on a six-month contract.

A wide variety of radio work followed during the next few years, including leading roles in classic serials such as *Wuthering Heights*, *The Forsyte Saga*, *War and Peace* and *Cold Comfort Farm*.

In addition to reading a large number of *Morning Story* scripts and serialised books on the radio, she was for some years a presenter of the much-missed *Listen with Mother*. She now lives near Warwick with her husband, Charles, and children, Tom and Harriet.

Apart from radio drama, she also does television and radio commercials, film and television commentaries, dubs foreign television serials and films into English, and works occasionally in television drama. In 1989 she was the voice of the star, Istara, in the children's BBC serial *Aliens in the Family*. She has also been involved in devising and presenting a number of poetry recitals.

The Archers is Pat's third radio soap opera. She has previously had roles in *The Dales* and *Waggoner's Walk*, where for a time she shared a flat with a character played by Rosalind Adams (Clarrie Grundy). She joined *The Archers* in 1974 as Pat Lewis and married Tony Archer later the same year. She hopes that Pat Archer is helping to increase public awareness of the organic farming movement, and that Bridge Farm will continue to prosper.

FRANCES GRAHAM (Helen Archer) joined *The Archers* in 1987 to become the Pony Club's keenest member. It was not exactly typecasting because her knowledge of horses extended only to distinguishing between the front and rear ends. She says the role of Helen Archer increased her equine vocabulary to phrases such as 'saddle' and 'gee-up'!

Born in 1974, Frances has always lived in real *Archers*-type territory. Presently attending the Alice Ottey School in Worcester, she has had acting experience in several Swan Theatre youth productions. However, as she is still in the middle of her GCSE courses, she does not see an acting career ahead of her just yet.

When she isn't acting or studying, Frances enjoys the normal pursuits of a teenager. These include watching *Neighbours* and, more unusually, the decorative technique of marbling. Horse-riding still does not feature in her list of hobbies.

Frances Graham (Helen Archer)

Patricia Gallimore (Pat Archer)

Patricia Greene (Jill Archer)

Mollie Harris
(Martha Woodford)

PATRICIA GREENE (Jill Archer) attended grammar school and studied at the Central School of Speech and Drama. She was one of the first actresses to go to Eastern Europe after the war. 'There were newspaper headlines about it,' she recalls. 'Actress flies behind Iron Curtain to play cow and that sort of thing.'

After that, she had a series of jobs – from bus conductress and waitress, to model and cook – but she always worked in the theatre whenever she could. 'In Wales once,' she says, 'I even blacked up and went on stage as a coal miner!'

At one point, she was invited to join the Rank Organisation as one of their starlets but, in the end, she didn't sign the contract. Instead, she concentrated on the theatre: the fringe in London with George Devine, and then Oxford Rep.

Her radio career started with *The Archers* in 1956. She has worked mainly on that ever since but still manages a few welcome forays into television and theatre. She especially enjoyed *The Archers* on

stage at the Watermill Theatre, Newbury. And she hopes very much to return to the theatre when her son goes to university and Jill Archer becomes less central in *The Archers* storyline.

MOLLIE HARRIS (Martha Woodford) started her BBC career as a writer, jotting down the stories and yarns she heard during nine years working on Oxfordshire farms during seedtime and harvest. She sent them to the producer of a programme called *In the Country*, introduced by Phil Drabble, and soon her voice became one of the best-known on Midland radio.

Later, some of her writings were accepted on other programmes, including *Regional Extra* (the Midlands opt-out from *Today*) and *The Countryside in . . . Spring, Summer, Autumn* and *Winter*.

After that, Mollie wrote her first book, *A Kind of Magic*, the highly acclaimed story of her childhood. She has been writing books ever since. The latest – and most successful – was *Cotswold Privies*, in 1988.

Brian Hewlett (Neil Carter)

Steve Hodson
(Martin Lambert)

Trevor Harrison (Eddie Grundy)

'I had an audition for radio plays back in the 1960s,' she remembers, 'but it was only in 1970 that I was given the part of Martha in *The Archers*.'

Mollie loves village life. She is a member of her local Women's Institute and talks to WI groups all over the country, always on country life and life in the village of her youth. She was a member of the parish council for nine years and has raised thousands of pounds for Cancer Research. Now she concentrates on raising money for a hospice, the Sir Michael Sobell House, at the Churchill Hospital in Oxford.

She has done a BBC Midlands television cookery series and also interviewed country folk on television. She now presents the programme *The Countryside in . . .* on BBC Radio 4, and often contributes items to her local radio station in Oxford. She loves gardening and makes gallons of home-made wine.

TREVOR HARRISON (Eddie Grundy) is a Stourbridge lad, as was Chriss Gittins (the actor who played the much-loved Walter Gabriel). Trevor went to the Birmingham Theatre School and then worked in repertory in Birmingham and Coventry, as well as doing a schools tour with Theatre in Education. After that came television, with appearances in *Get Some In*, *Hazel* and *Stig of the Dump*, and he has been spotted drinking and chatting up girls in an advert for Harp lager. Children know him from *Jackanory*, *Playhouse* and *The*

Basil Brush Show and for his reading of stories on Radio 4's *Listening Corner*.

It is his characterisation of Eddie Grundy, though, that has bought him dazzling fame, four record releases and his very own fan club. It has also made him wary about coincidences.

As he tells it: 'In one episode, Eddie was kicked by a cow and the night the episode was broadcast a herd of cows surrounded my car in a country lane and kicked it hard. On another occasion, Eddie's van broke down in the programme, and the same day my own vehicle came to a halt.'

'The greatest coincidence, though, started at The White Bear hotel in Shipston-on-Stour, where the *Radio Times* took publicity pictures of Clarrie and Eddie's wedding reception, pretending it was The Bull, where Clarrie was the barmaid.

A year later I went back to The White Bear for a fan-club reunion, started chatting to the barmaid, Julia Cook, and now I'm married to her!'

Trevor and Julia live in Leamington Spa . . . when they're not travelling round the country so that Trevor can close things down. 'Other actors get asked to open things but I keep being asked to close things, like a store in Oxford Street and a festival in Salisbury. It's funny, that!'

He has also enjoyed hosting the Radio 2 *Country Club* programme.

BRIAN HEWLETT (Neil Carter) trained at the Rose Bruford College in Kent, and first trod the boards 30 years ago at London's Mermaid Theatre in *Lock Up Your Daughters*. Since then, his work has taken him to theatres throughout the land; to television studios in Manchester, Birmingham, and London; to film studios in Elstree; and, of course, to the hallowed halls of Broadcasting House and Pebble Mill.

Radio has figured largely in his career. He has been with the BBC Radio Drama Company on four long-term contracts (encompassing hundreds of plays) and his freelance work has included the notorious Widmerpool in Anthony Powell's *A Dance to the Music of Time* (a 12-novel opus broadcast periodically over four years). He has played the part of Neil Carter since his first appearance in Ambridge in 1973.

Musicals have always featured in Brian's theatrical career, and some of the roles he has enjoyed performing most have been Amos Hart in *Chicago* (in London's West End), Herr Schultz in *Cabaret* (at Coventry and Salisbury), and Tevye in *Fiddler on the Roof* (at Ipswich). 'I'm very lucky,' he says, 'to be in the kind of work to move people to tears or to laughter . . . the kind of work which entertains.'

Brian is also an amateur naturalist and photographer who cares deeply about the environment and the need to conserve wildlife. He has been lucky enough to spend some holidays experiencing the wilder parts of the world at first hand . . . in Peru, Kenya and Rwanda (where he observed rare mountain gorillas). But he also takes great pleasure in wildlife nearer home – he lives in an old farmhouse and the overgrown orchard and pond serve as his own wildlife garden.

STEVE HODSON (Martin Lambert) spent three years at the Central School of Speech and Drama before going to work for the late, great director Michael Elliott at Manchester '69 (now the Manchester Exchange) in 1970. While playing Lysander in *A Midsummer Night's Dream*, he was offered a role in a television play, *The Grievance*, directed by Alan Cooke. He was then asked to be in Cooke's next play on television, *The Rivals of Sherlock Holmes*. The two roles he played were very different and very exciting for a young actor – those of a skinhead and a Victorian gentleman.

This was followed by a three-month contract at Yorkshire Television, to do a children's series called *Follyfoot*. The three months turned into a very happy three and a half years! However, he feels that perhaps he spent too much time doing television too early and therefore became rather disaffected with it.

When he was offered his first radio play he fell in love with a medium that allowed him to play so many different parts, parts that he couldn't possibly play on the stage or on television: 'Radio's immediacy, the necessity for ensemble-playing and the fact that one had only two days to record a one-hour play, a process demanding much preparation . . . even homework, thrilled me and does to this day. For example, in one eight-day period, I played a black African guerrilla leader educated at Oxford, a seventeenth-century fop and Adolf Hitler!'

This led to the Radio Repertory Company and the happiest 18 months of his life: 'Directors used to ask me as a young actor, what I really wanted to play, expecting the answer Hamlet or Coriolanus. My answer was Walter Gabriel! I doubt that it did me any good at all but if Martin Lambert is around for the next 30 years, he and I may just begin to sound like Walter!'

ROGER HUME (Bert Fry) began his career in the theatre as an assistant stage manager at Wimbledon Theatre and worked his way through various back-stage jobs before becoming an actor. He was a flying-wire operator with *The Crazy Gang*, he worked with Kenneth Williams in one of the *Carry On* films,. and the never-to-be-forgotten – Bing Crosby, Bob Hope, Dean Martin and Frank Sinatra – in *Road to the Moon*.

He spent three years in a teacher training college before returning to the stage, since when he has played leading roles with most of the principal repertory companies in the country and small parts with the Royal Shakespeare Company at Stratford. In London, he appeared at the Royal Court Theatre in the original productions of *Teeth 'n' Smiles* and Edward Bond's *The Fool*, in a revival of *Blithe Spirit* at the Vaudeville and in *The Resistible Rise of Artura Ui* at the Queen's Theatre.

In 1979, he created the part of Herbert Pinnegar in Alfred Shaughnessy's one-man play, *Old Herbaceous*, first at Salisbury Playhouse and later when it transferred to the Mayfair Theatre in London for a highly acclaimed season. He later recorded it for television and radio and toured with it round Australia and the UK, as well as Zimbabwe and the Charleston Festival in South Carolina.

His television work includes leading parts in *Special Branch*, *Play for Today*, *The Headmasters* and *Family Man*, and appearances in *Coronation Street*, *Edward and Mrs Simpson*, *Rumpole of the Bailey*, *Fawlty Towers*, *God's Wonderful Railway*, *The Bill*, *Hercule Poirot's Casebook* and *EastEnders*.

Among other films, he has appeared in *The Offence* and *Car Trouble*. And if you blink you'll miss him in John Cleese's *A Fish Called Wanda*!

As well as *The Archers*, Roger works regularly in radio plays, documentaries and reading stories, some of which he writes himself. Like most working actors these days he also spends a good deal of time making corporate training videos.

He has written and compiled two one-man shows: *Winston*, a portrait of Sir Winston Churchill in old age; and *Please Sir*, a humorous look at school life from the teacher's point of view. He has also co-written a play with Richard Derrington (Mark Hebden) called *The Campden Wonder*, based on events that took place in the seventeenth century in south Warwickshire, near where he lives with his wife and two sons.

Bert Fry is Roger's third role in *The Archers*. For two years, in the early eighties, he played John Tregorran, and he also appeared at one of Jack Woolley's shooting parties as Sir Sidney Goodman.

EDWARD KELSEY (Joe Grundy) left the RAF in 1951, trained at the Royal Academy of Music and graduated as a teacher of speech and drama. He also won the Howard de Walden Gold Medal and was winner of the Carlton Hobbs Radio Award in its second year. 'Since then, radio has always been my first love,' he says, 'although I've been involved in most other branches of the acting profession.'

His first theatre work was in the tour of *Reluctant Heroes* and that was followed by many years in rep, notably at Guildford. He has made a number of television appearances over the years, including the BBC series *Campion*. In a very different context, he also provides the voices of Baron Greenback and Col. K in the cartoon series *Dangermouse*!

Ted does a great deal of writing and presenting for BBC Schools Radio, and has just finished the book and lyrics of a new musical version of *Aladdin*.

GRAEME KIRK (Kenton Archer) was born in Crowborough in Sussex, educated at Sunbury-on-Thames and trained at the Drama Centre, London. The highlight of his amateur theatrical career was accepting the Laurence Olivier Drama Award of the National Association of Boys' Clubs on behalf of Heatham House Youth Theatre. It was presented by Geraldine McEwan. After that, Graeme joined Michael Croft's National Youth Theatre for

Roger Hume
(Bert Fry)

Edward Kelsey
(Joe Grundy)

Graeme Kirk
(Kenton Archer)

Crawford Logan
(Matthew Thorogood)

a tour of West Germany and the London productions of *Zigger Zagger* and *Macbeth*.

Having completed three years' training at drama school, he was forced to change his surname from Bond to Kirk because there was another Equity member called Graeme Bond. In this new guise, he toured with Brian Way's Theatre Centre and then spent two very enjoyable years with Peter Cheeseman's Victoria Theatre, Stoke-on-Trent, appearing in over a dozen productions.

The other theatres where he has worked include the Phoenix and Haymarket, Leicester; the Duke's Playhouse, Lancaster; and the Liverpool Playhouse, where he appeared as David in the very successful production of *Blood on the Dole*, which transferred to the Tricycle Theatre, London.

Before joining *The Archers*, Graeme had twice toured the premier theatres in Scotland with the Borderline Theatre Company's sell-out production of Dario Fo's *Trumpets and Raspberries*. His television roles include Jack in episodes of *Brookside*; Ralph Ward in *Coronation Street*; and Dave in the BBC series *Seaview*.

His leisure pursuits are golf, cricket and spending time at home in Lancaster or in the beautiful north-west countryside with his wife, Bobbie, and their young son, Jack.

Graeme says his similarities with Kenton include gambling, an inability to slice bread and complete ignorance about farming!

CRAWFORD LOGAN (Matthew Thorogood) is in his second incarnation in *The Archers*. Some years ago he played a former boyfriend of Caroline Bone, the mysterious ex-SAS man, Alan Fraser. For those with even longer memories, he also played the hardbitten Glaswegian news editor, Maurice Gill, in the late-lamented *Waggoner's Walk*.

Although he has developed a considerable career in radio, he has also worked in theatre and television. Most notably, he played Detective Sergeant Trotter in *The Mousetrap*, and appeared in Tom Stoppard's *Dirty Linen*, both in the West End.

On television, he particularly enjoyed filming *Secret Army* in Brussels, where his fair hair and SS uniform caused so much unrest that several locals had to be removed by the police. He has also appeared in *EastEnders*, as a nasty loan shark.

Crawford was born in Scotland, where he has recently returned with his wife and two young children. As a train addict, he finds travelling to Birmingham to record *The Archers* a great pleasure as the seasons go by. In fact, he's very keen on travel generally, one of his favourite trips being a journey to China by train, via Mongolia, at the end of the Cultural Revolution. As a result he very much enjoys cooking Chinese meals.

He is an equally keen – though not always very successful – golfer, as well as being one of the most loyal supporters of Stirling Albion FC. And perhaps he *ought* to do a first-aid course . . .

CHARLOTTE MARTIN (Susan Carter, née Horrobin) was born in Fontainebleau, near Paris, where her father was working at NATO Headquarters. And she grew up at the family home in Solihull.

At the age of three, she went to dancing school; when she was nine she took the lead in *Babooshka*, a Christmas play; and at secondary school she was in every play that was staged. After school, she successfully auditioned for the Birmingham Theatre School, where she gained a Licentiate Diploma in Drama from the Guildhall School of Music.

After leaving drama school, she appeared as the maid in *The Importance of Being Earnest* at Birmingham Repertory Theatre and shortly afterwards auditioned for *The Archers*. As well as thoroughly enjoying playing Susan, Charlotte appears in numerous *Afternoon Theatre* and *Saturday Night Theatre* productions for Radio 4. These have included *Lark Rise to Candleford*, *Family Membership*, *The Golden Ass* and *The Brothers Karamazov*.

On television, Charlotte has appeared in *Crossroads*, *Boon* and *A Very Peculiar Practice*, among others. She has also made a pop video for the group UB40. Having trained as a dancer, she spends her spare time choreographing and, occasionally, teaching. She also writes short stories and poetry.

JACK MAY (Nelson Gabriel) says his education was excellent: 'I got it somewhere between Evelyn Waugh's *Decline and Fall* and Warwick Deeping's *Sorell and Son!*'

Born in Henley-on-Thames, he knew from childhood that he was destined for an extrovert career: 'Barrister, archbishop, prime minister – Mrs Thatcher could have been my Chancellor of the Exchequer – or quite possibly the theatre.'

He spent the war in India, came back and taught for a year, before going on to Merton College, Oxford. After that, he got a job at the Birmingham Repertory Theatre and stayed there for four years. 'With the exception of Paul Schofield, I stayed there longer than any other actor.'

Jack was the first actor to play Henry, consecutively, in the three parts of *Henry VI*. That was at the Old Vic in 1954. Between 1955 and 1985, he says modestly that he was employed as a jobbing actor. In reality, that means numerous film roles, leading parts in the West End, 25 television serials and hundreds of radio plays. He has been in both versions of *Goodbye Mr Chips* and he is the only actor to have played both Julius Caesar and Octavius Caesar in a major production at the Old Vic.

Jack is very fond of Nelson Gabriel: 'He's not a crook but he is a bit of a rogue.' He feels that there is a bit of Nelson in him but says that listeners imagine him as being tall, dark and handsome. 'When they see this wizened geriatric they get a bit of a shock!'

Other credits of which Jack is particularly proud include *The Verdict is Yours* (Granada TV), a live unscripted series (the predecessor of *Crown Court*); *Spread of the Eagle*; and *Age of Kings*, directed by Peter Dews for the BBC.

More recently, he has been heard as the voice of Igor, the butler, in *Count Duckula*; he also played a drunken vicar in *All Creatures Great and Small*. And, in September 1989, he played Captain Wragge in a Radio 4 play called *No Name*, produced by Janet Whittaker.

Charlotte Martin (Susan Carter)

TERRY MOLLOY (Mike Tucker) started his career in repertory, working at theatres like Birmingham Repertory, Coventry Belgrade, Stoke-on-Trent's Victoria Theatre, the Liverpool Playhouse, Leicester's Haymarket, the Cambridge Theatre and Greenwich. He also did the national tour of *Godspell* and several tours with the Prospect Theatre Company, including a visit to the Edinburgh Festival.

Terry has been making more and more appearances on television in recent years, with guest roles in *EastEnders*, *Crossroads*, *Connie* and *Bergerac*; in a number of one-off plays, including *The Exercise*, *The Index Has Gone Fishing*, and *All Together Now!*; and in several major series, including *Oliver Twist*, *Radio Phoenix* and *Vote for Them*.

His most recent credits have been as Harry English, in Channel 4's *The Real Eddy English*, and as Bob Lomax in Central's *Tales of Sherwood Forest*. He is also the face behind the mask of Davros, creator of the daleks in *Dr Who*, and a member of the 'hit squad' for London Weekend Television's *Beadle's About*.

Terry is perhaps best known for his radio work, with over 300 radio plays, numerous readings of *Book at Bedtime* and *Morning Story*, and many documentaries to his credit. These include his reading of *Saturday Night and Sunday Morning*, lead roles in *Precious Bane*, *The Old Wives' Tale*, *Adam Bede*, and *Risky City*, for which he received the Pye Radio Award for Best Actor in 1981. He has been playing the part of Mike Tucker in *The Archers* since 1972.

Terry is a committed Christian and an active member of his church. He is married to Heather Barrett (formerly Dorothy Adamson in *The Archers*) and they live in Birmingham with their three children. His son, Philip, plays William Grundy in *The Archers*. In his spare time, he runs a film production company making corporate training films.

CELIA NELSON (Sharon Richards) was born in Cardiff and lived there until she was seven years old. Her family then moved to the West Sussex resort of Worthing where, between summers on the beach, she continued her education.

Jack May (Nelson Gabriel)

Terry Molloy (Mike Tucker)

Celia Nelson (Sharon Richards)

She pursued her career in drama with a three-year course at the Webber Douglas Academy and, soon after leaving, she got her first professional role in *Playboy of the Western World*, at the Torch Theatre, Milford Haven. Her next five roles were also in Wales . . . as the nurse in *A Streetcar Named Desire* and Glorvina in *Vanity Fair* at the Sherman Theatre, Cardiff; Eleanor in *Turn the Old Year Go*, Violet in *Charlie and the Chocolate Factory*, and in *Hard Times*, again at the Torch Theatre.

Celia said she was delighted to join *The Archers*, a firm favourite of hers for many years. She feels the role of Sharon has huge potential, despite her being in dire straits at present, and she hopes the casting of such a contemporary character will encourage a younger following for the programme.

HEDLI NIKLAUS (Kathy Perks) studied drama at the University of California where she learned the Method school of acting by pretending to be a jelly and making jelly noises with the department's 'jelly congregation'!

Back in England, she took a more conventional degree in drama at Manchester University and started her professional acting career with Brian Way's touring company in schools throughout England and Scotland. Since then, she has been in rep all over the country including Torquay, where she met her husband, actor Leon Tanner.

She has been in many radio and television plays and presented the Tyne-Tees Television series, *Look-Out*. Kathy Perks is Hedli's third character in *The Archers*. Her first appearance was as Libby Jones, a milk-recorder, and she later returned as Eva Lenz, the Home Farm au pair. That was when she married her husband for the second time – he was then playing PC Jim Coverdale, who married Eva and took her away from Ambridge!

Hedli works for the charity Books for Children, often presents *Listening Corner* and is a member of Terry Trower's company, Pied Piper, which tells musical stories for children. She has two children of her own, Nick and Kate, and lives in Warwickshire.

ARNOLD PETERS (Jack Woolley) began his broadcasting career with a *Children's Hour* programme called *Hastings of Bengal* in 1951. He has now clocked up over 3000 radio programmes and 250 television appearances, and has been in several feature films.

After serving in the RAF he started acting at the Royal Theatre, Northampton, and spent five years in weekly and fortnightly rep. He then began to get work with the BBC, and was a member of the BBC Drama Company in Birmingham in the early 1950s. In 1953, he joined *The Archers* to play Len Thomas. When Len was written out, he played the Reverend David Latimer and after the demise of the Reverend Latimer, he took a break from Ambridge until 1980, when he returned as Jack Woolley. Arnold's only complaint is that, on meeting him, listeners have been known to say: 'I thought you'd be shorter and fatter than you are!'

Arnold lives in the East Midlands, where he has written and directed several pantomimes and directed musicals, including several by Gilbert and Sullivan. He is also very involved with the

Hedli Niklaus (Kathy Perks)

Arnold Peters (Jack Woolley)

Angela Piper (Jennifer Aldridge)

Physically Handicapped and Able-Bodied charity (PHAB).

He is married with one daughter, Caroline, who teaches ballet at a London stage school. His hobbies include painting, dancing and music, and he is a member of a folk dance band.

ANGELA PIPER (Jennifer Aldridge) unwittingly upset a listener who wrote very severely about her to Brian Aldridge, at Home Farm, Ambridge: 'I know you do not realise it, but your wife Jennifer is secretly visiting London to read letters on BBC television's *Points of View*. You must stop this. She is taking work away from a qualified person and cannot possibly need the money.'

Actress Angela ('Who says I don't need the money?') must have upset that correspondent even

more if he saw her in Yorkshire Television's *Life Begins at Forty* and *Third Time Lucky*, not to mention several television commercials, lots of film voice-overs and a stage appearance at the Belgrade Theatre, Coventry.

Angela trained for the stage at the Royal Academy of Music, where she won the broadcasting prize. After that came the theatre, working as an assistant stage manager and playing juvenile leads, more radio work and eventually the part of rebellious young schoolgirl, Jennifer Archer.

Apart from acting, Angela also adjudicates at music and drama festivals, gives poetry readings, opens fêtes up and down the country and – with her television announcer husband, Peter – looks after three children in a house surrounded by dogs, cats, chickens, ducks, geese, a rabbit and a guinea pig.

Lesley Saweard
(Christine Archer)

Graham Roberts
(George Barford)

GRAHAM ROBERTS (George Barford) was born in Chester. His father was Welsh, and his mother's family moved from Edinburgh, through South Yorkshire, to Cheshire.

Graham was educated at King's School, Chester; Manchester and Bristol Universities; and at the Bristol Old Vic Theatre School. His National Service was spent in the Royal Navy.

He is the first member of his family to enter the theatrical profession but, even as a child, he showed a talent for music and drama, spending most of his time off the sports field performing in shows . . . or watching them!

His first professional engagement was with the Arena Theatre touring out of Birmingham; then followed repertory at St Andrews, Edinburgh, Perth, Whitby, Manchester, Oldham and Liverpool. Graham appeared in the world premiere of

Eric Linklater's *Breakspear in Gascony* at the Edinburgh Festival, in the royal performance of Goldoni's *Venetian Twins* and in the Indian government's production of Tagore's *Red Oleanders*. He also toured Italy in the Old Vic production of Ben Jonson's *The Alchemist*. His West End plays include *Poor Horace*, *Samson*, *The Wild Duck* and *Bristow*.

He has appeared in the feature films *This Sporting Life*, *A Taste of Honey* and *A Touch of Brass*, and among his many television appearances are PC Aitken in *Z Cars*, Mr Mayor in *Lizzie Dripping* and *Adam Smith*.

It's in radio, however, that Graham has really made his mark. His vocal range and variety of dialects have taken him from children's plays to *Saturday Night Theatre*, and from *Morning Story* to Radio 3 drama. Graham has also introduced *Your Concert*

Choice on Radio 3 and is a continuity announcer for Yorkshire Television.

He is married to Dame Isobel Baillie's protégée, the soprano, Yvonne Robert. And one of their joint successes is a series of anthologies of words and music, with which they make several tours a year.

LESLEY SAWEARD (Christine Archer) recalls that she was working as a teacher in 1953 when she met the late Denis Folwell, who played Jack Archer, and he remarked on how similar her voice was to that of Pamela Mant, the girl who was then playing Christine Archer. 'I had been trained as an actress, so I jokingly said that if she left, he should let me know, little realising how that chance remark was to change the whole course of my life.'

Pamela Mant did leave the programme shortly afterwards, and Lesley was called to Birmingham for an audition. She got the part and the voice match with Pamela was so complete that hardly anyone noticed the change. 'I've been playing Christine ever since,' says Lesley, 'apart from the years when my two children were born.'

Lesley has made many public appearances as Chris over the years and particularly remembers being given a standing ovation by members of the Women's Institute at the Albert Hall; and being very moved when a blind man presented her with the first thing he had made since losing his sight.

Another memorable time was when the programme adopted a young show-jumper named Red Link and followed its qualifying progress round the shows, finally appearing at The Horse of the Year Show in the finals of the Foxhunter competition. It was ridden by top rider, Alan Oliver, but, sadly, did not win. The consolation for Lesley was patting the famous show-jumper, Foxhunter, himself.

Lesley met her husband, Geoffrey Lewis, in *The Archers*, when he was playing one of his many parts, Dr Cavendish. Sarah, their 22-year-old daughter, like Chris, is a qualified riding instructor, now working in Devon.

Lesley once opened a fête for farmer Henry Burt, whose idea of a farming *Dick Barton* was the inspiration for the programme. She also stayed at the home of Henry and his wife, Christine, after whom her character was named.

Apart from *The Archers*, Lesley works in many areas, from taped novels to voice-overs and from *Morning Story* to reading letters on *Points of View*.

PAULINE SEVILLE (Mrs Perkins) trained at the Royal Academy of Dramatic Art and her first job was with the Manchester Repertory Company, where the leading man was Noel Johnson, the original Dick Barton. In 1943, she went into the Entertainments National Service Association (ENSA), entertaining the troops all over Britain and, later, in Germany. More repertory work followed, at Leicester and Newcastle, and then with Hilton Edwards' Dublin Gate Theatre Company at the Vaudeville Theatre in London.

Her radio work has included *Children's Hour* plays, and *Guilty Party*, which was written by *Archers* scriptwriters, Edward J. Mason and Geoffrey Webb. The part of Mrs Perkins came Pauline's way after her audition was heard by Godfrey Baseley.

Pauline Seville (Mrs Perkins – weeding in the garden, Spring 1954).

Pauline has not only played Mrs Perkins from the earliest days of the programme, but she has also taken the parts of Rita Flynn and a girl called Audrey, who used to clean for John Tregorran.

Married to a retired master-printer, she has a son and a daughter.

COLIN SKIPP (Tony Archer) started writing scripts with actor, Victor Maddern, while working as an office boy with the Rank Organisation and he determined to earn his living from the theatre. 'Then my country called me,' he says, 'and I spent two years as a private in the Pay Corps.' His National Service was not without distinction as he was one of a dozen privates selected to form a new 'Electronic Accounting Development Unit' – to test out something called a computer!

Colin Skipp (Tony Archer – chatting to Walter Gabriel (Chris Gittins), 1968).

After his army service, Colin won a scholarship to the Royal Academy of Dramatic Art and worked his way through by washing dishes at the Lyon's Corner House in Oxford Circus. 'I became hooked on washing up,' he laughs, 'starting with all those messy dishes and ending up with everything clean, neat and tidy . . . a perfect performance every time!' Colin still does the washing-up at his home in St Anne's on Sea.

After winning the RADA fencing prize and the BBC drama student prize, he went into rep and it was while doing a summer season at Guernsey in 1968 that he met his wife-to-be, actress Lisa Davies.

By then, he was appearing in television serials like *United* and *The Newcomers*, had been in the West End revival of *The Long and the Short and the Tall* and had been heard playing a schoolboy in a radio play.

'I was asked to audition for 16-year-old Tony Archer and, although I was nearly 30 at the time I got the part.' The age gap, he says, has had some amusing repercussions. 'When I got married in 1970, one newspaper confused my age with that of Tony Archer and reported that Lisa was marrying an 18-year-old actor. All her friends thought she was cradle-snatching.'

Away from *The Archers*, Colin has become well known as a stage director for such companies as Triumph Productions, David Gordon Productions and Tom Edwards Promotions. He is also the in-house director of Centenary Players Productions. 'I enjoy directing so much because there's no limit to what I can achieve,' says Colin. 'As an actor I obviously have limitations but as a director, I can aim for the moon!'

DAVID VANN (Detective Sergeant Dave Barry) was born on 12 January 1951 – just 11 days after *The Archers* was first broadcast nationally – and he confesses that as a teenager he rapidly acquired a taste for drinking beer at The Old Bull at Inkberrow, the pub on which The Bull in Ambridge is said to have been based. 'Other contact with Ambridge remained purely that of a listener until 1981, when Sergeant Barry arrived at Borchester nick,' he says.

In the meantime, David studied for an English

David Vann (Dave Barry)

Tracy-Jane White (Lucy Perks)

degree at the University of East Anglia (where he spent most of his time with the dramatic society), then trained at the London Academy of Music and Dramatic Art, before launching into his career as a professional actor.

His stage appearances include roles as varied as a punk Ugly Sister in the pantomine *Cinderella*, Squire Blackheart in *The Thwarting of Baron Bolligrew*, and Mr Brown in *The Adventures of Paddington Bear*. He has spent a season with the Chichester Festival Theatre and played in two productions at the National Theatre. More recently had has worked at the Swan Theatre, Worcester; and has also directed several plays including *The Relapse*, *As You Like It*, and *Hess* for a national tour.

Television viewers have seen him in *The Professionals* and the play, *Easy Money*, in the BBC *Playhouse* series, and he has taken many roles in radio plays.

TRACY-JANE WHITE (Lucy Perks) has played the wayward teenager since 1982 and her father in real life, as well as in *The Archers*, is Alan Devereux (Sid Perks).

Most of her work has been in television and her credits include, *All Creatures Great and Small* (BBC), *Shadow of the Noose* (BBC), *No Frills* (BBC), *Stolen* (LWT), and *High Street Blues* (LWT).

Tracy-Jane has also taken part in *Songs of Praise* in which she professed her faith as a Christian and said it was the most important thing in her life. She is married to Steve, an electronics engineer, and they live near London with their dog, Beth.

Nicola Wright (Rosemary Tarrant)

NICOLA WRIGHT (Rosemary Tarrant) began her career as an actress in Sidmouth in weekly rep. Since then, her stage work has included a national tour playing Wendy in *Peter Pan*; Laura in *The Glass Menagerie*; Diaphanta in *The Changeling*; two pantomimes at the New Theatre, Cardiff (where she also worked as assistant director on *Robin Hood*); and Peter in Kenneth Branagh's production of *Romeo and Juliet*.

Among her television credits are Clarita in *Christabel*, Adina in Screen 2's *Border*, Nurse Cath in *Still Life*, Ruth in *Desert of Lies*, Cam in *To the Lighthouse*, and Rosie Spencer in *Grange Hill* (all for the BBC). She has also appeared in *Dick Turpin*, Channel 4's film *Remembrance*, *Just a Game*, and a thriller video series called *Mystery Tour*.

Nicola's film credits include *Top Secret*, *Burning an Illusion*, *Lamb*, *Man's Recreation* and *We Think the World of You*. She has also worked as a dancer on stage and in television, and as a choreographer for Welsh television. She first joined the cast of *The Archers* three years ago, when she turned up on Nelson's doorstep as his daughter, Rosemary.

CHAPTER FOUR

THE EDITORS

FOR THE FIRST 20 years, the *Archers* production team consisted of an editor, a producer, two writers, a programme assistant and a secretary. Between them, this close-knit group produced more than 5000 episodes . . . a record of achievement that can surely never be equalled again.

Of that team, two members worked throughout the period: editor Godfrey Baseley and writer Edward J. Mason. A third man, producer Tony Shryane, went on to complete 28 years with the programme. After them have come Malcolm Lynch (1972–73), Charles Lefeaux (1973–78), William Smethurst (1978–86), Liz Rigbey (1986–89) and the present editor, Ruth Patterson.

Editing a long-running daily serial must be one of the toughest jobs in broadcasting. It was, perhaps, summed up in the 1989 advertisement for a new editor:

Can you handle seven million bosses? **The Archers** *is the world's longest-running serial and each week it attracts about seven million listeners . . . most of whom know about the twists and turns of the storyline and all the nuances of the characters almost as well as the writers and production team. They also care just as much.*

Now we're looking for an editor to take the programme into the 1990s – together with its seven million listeners, and perhaps a few more.

You'll need to know exactly what we're talking about; you'll need courage, resilience, a sense of humour and total commitment; you'll need to believe that actors are the most important people on earth . . . and be able to explain that away to the writers and to the production staff, not to mention your boss!

All of the programme's editors have measured up to these demands in their different ways and all have made lasting contributions towards keeping *The Archers* a firm favourite with the listeners.

The production team (c. 1954) . . . Tony Shryane, Godfrey Baseley, Edward J. Mason and Geoffrey Webb escape from the rigours of producing and writing for this day in the country.

First among them – in every sense – must be Godfrey Baseley, the man who invented it all. He only stayed on for a few months after I became managerially responsible for the programme, so I never really got to know him personally. But I knew his reputation, and that was formidable.

He had single-handedly fought those that scorned the idea of using drama to tell the world about the farmer's problems in those grim post-war days of food-rationing. It took more than two years of bombarding his bosses with memos and telephone calls before they finally gave in. Indeed, folklore had it that Godfrey intimidated the gentlemen of the BBC establishment into agreeing to let him produce his Dick-Barton-of-the-farmyard so that they could have a quiet life.

When I arrived on the scene, everything about Godfrey's demeanour lent credence to the myth. In his book, *Forever Ambridge*, Norman Painting describes him as 'fearsome' and he wasn't far wrong. Godfrey had a deep bass voice and spoke – some might say bellowed – with the total commitment and conviction of the fanatic. He was clearly unassailed by anything as wimpish as self-doubt. At 67 (seven years beyond the BBC's normal retirement age), *The Archers* was very much his castle and followed his own design. The astonishing long-term success of his creation added to his obstinacy in the face of critical comment or suggestions for improvement from any Johnny-come-lately. That he held total sway was never in any doubt. He was the Squire and he didn't tolerate fools at all, let alone gladly.

It didn't take me long to find my place in his firmament. I was not only a fool but a townie as well. His contempt was as powerful as it was obvious.

I have since learned that it's not all that unusual for minor bosses to be treated that way in the BBC but, to someone as green as I was then, it came as quite a shock. I'm not quite sure what I expected when I was appointed out of the blue and unceremoniously dumped on the group of highly creative and vastly experienced programme-makers that made up the network radio unit in Birmingham, but it certainly wasn't the animosity that greeted my appearance in the *Archers'* office. While all the other producers showed a cool politeness at their new boss's arrival, Godfrey was uncompromising. He didn't want me interfering.

It would be dishonest to say I didn't react badly to being told I ought to keep my nose out of things. What he didn't know was that I had been told by the managing director of radio that the programme was so much in the doldrums that it was likely to be taken off the air within months. I felt I had to get involved and, in my inexperience, I decided to fight fire with fire. I met Godfrey head-on. When he insisted that he should run *The Archers* his way, I pointed out that my masters were insisting on changes and that changes there would be!

Godfrey Baseley, the creator and first editor of The Archers, *single-handedly fought those who scorned the idea of using drama to inform farmers about new ideas.*

With hindsight, I know I should have handled it differently. I honestly believe that Godfrey and I could have made a great team and that we could have resolved all the programme's difficulties amicably. Sadly, I allowed my newly inflated ego to get the better of me. Because he wouldn't listen to me, I refused to listen to him. It was a mistake that I have regretted for all of the past 20 years because the outcome was that he left the programme he had created in a blaze of anger instead of the blaze of glory he so richly deserved.

Again, in my inexperience, I didn't at first recognise the deep hurt he felt and by the time I did, he was in no mood for reconciliation. Over the years I have seen my olive branches shrivel in the heat of his continuing contempt.

I could never blame him because I knew that, as he saw it, I had snatched away his beloved programme and was using it for my own ends. In his view, I was currying favour with my boss and exploiting *The Archers* to further my career. I had not been party to the programme's creation, nor to the building of its success, and yet there I was trying to show *him* how it should be done. In his position, I'm sure I would have been positively apoplectic.

Set against that background, you can imagine how my heart sank when he finally accepted the invitation to attend the celebrations marking the ten thousandth episode in May 1989. I had assumed that, as on previous occasions, he would have sent a rather cool apology.

On the night, both of us were clearly making an effort, being terribly British and trying not to create an atmosphere that would spoil the occasion for other people. Happily, I soon found that my long-standing respect and admiration for him overcame any juvenile resentment. When the time came to propose the toast to our guests, I was able to put into words just how much we owed him and Tony Shryane for the success of the programme. They were given a standing ovation that lasted long enough to move strong men to tears. It was a great moment . . . but for me, there was more to come. A few days later I got a letter from Godfrey. It read:
Although our relationship in the past has not always been one of accord, on this occasion I am delighted to be able to congratulate you on your skill and organisational capacity to stage such a wonderful event as the 10 000 celebration event last night. It was something I shall never forget, and both Tony and myself were very proud to hear your remarks that brought about such a spontaneous standing ovation.

Never in my wildest dreams did I ever expect **The Archers** *to have survived and to have retained its popularity for such a long time.*

The pattern of the programme has changed and so has life and work in the rural areas. I only have to compare the village I came to live in some 25 years ago with what it is like today. From a truly rural community it has, over the years, become a dormitory for commuters and even I, as the oldest inhabitant, am considered to be something of a character as I tootle around on my tricycle.

My reply shows just how I felt:
I can't tell you how delighted I was to receive your note. Twenty years is much too long for two souls to be in conflict and I'm thrilled that we can put all that behind us. It was a very generous gesture on your part and one which I very much appreciate. It was good to see you at the ten thousandth celebrations and I meant every word of my comments in recognition of your work in creating and establishing **The Archers** *so successfully. I was not surprised by the standing ovation: it was the natural way for everyone to show you their deep respect and affection. It was a special part of a very special evening.*

The reasons for publishing this exchange are not just to underline the stature of the man who was able to make the first move in ending years of bitterness but to publicly right any wrongs that I might have been responsible for over the years . . . wrongs that were sneaky sins of omission rather than commission. It's true that I have never tried to take anything away from Godfrey, but at the same time I was hardly fulsome about him in the various books we've published since he left the programme in 1971.

No one should now be in any doubt that it was Godfrey Baseley, more than anyone, who set the standards that have helped to sustain the programme over so many years. And it was his unflagging commitment to farmers and farming

Tony Shryane was the first producer and the guiding light of the programme for 28 years. Watching him in the studio was like sitting in on Masterclass.

that underpinned the essential agricultural content from the first script right through to today.

He was clearly a disciplinarian, and his insistance on accuracy and sense of purpose in every script, every characterisation, every performance has rubbed off either directly or indirectly on everyone associated with the programme. Perhaps not all of us have been prepared to admit it out loud but we know it in the deep recesses of our conscience.

The other single greatest influence on *The Archers* has been Tony Shryane, the producer for more than a quarter of a century. While Godfrey pursued his high-profile style of management, Tony dealt with all the minutiae of the everyday story of countryfolk. He and Godfrey were like chalk and cheese. Tony was quietly spoken and gentle. In all the time I worked with him, I never saw him lose his temper or get upset. I think he felt that energy was squandered if it wasn't applied single-mindedly to the job in hand.

At the same time, he was certainly afflicted by the Baseley accuracy bug. As he saw it, the job was simply to translate the scripts into the best kind of radio. He was therefore meticulous in getting the right sound effects, creating the rural atmosphere, and in bringing the best out of his actors and actresses. Watching him in the studio was like sitting in on a master class. He watched over his programme like a hawk watching its prey. His sharp eye – and ear – missed nothing. He was never happy unless every pause for breath was in exactly the right place and every word was said with the proper intonation. He never relaxed his standards.

One day, for example, the script included a scene where one of the cattle was being treated for warble fly. To the town-dweller, this is a fairly gruesome business that entails using a very stiff bristle brush to scrub out the sore where the warble has burrowed into the animal's hide. The sound effects man thought Tony might settle for the noise of a scrubbing brush on a piece of coconut-matting. He was wrong. Tony scoffed at the artificiality of the resulting sound and insisted that only a real cow would do.

At some inconvenience to himself, the studio manager travelled from the studio in built-up Birmingham deep into rural Worcestershire where he somehow persuaded a bewildered farmer to scrub down his cow with a stiff brush while the sound was duly recorded. Back at the studio, his initiative was greeted with: 'Good . . . but are you sure the cow did have warble fly?'

The same sound man, John Pierce, went on to record more than 4000 other effects that gave Tony Shryane the most comprehensive library of country and farmyard noises in the world. To this day, most of the storylines sent out to the writers include the exhortation to make use of the sound effects to create the right atmosphere.

In the best traditions of the BBC, Tony was inordinately polite, treated his secretaries with great courtesy and always wore a suit . . . but behind that correct image lay a tremendous sense of humour and a delicious sense of fun. How else would he have been able to devise – with *Archers* colleague, Edward J. Mason – those brilliant and long-running radio programmes, *My Word* and *My Music*, which feature the wit and wisdom of Denis Norden and Frank Muir?

This side of Tony's character was just as important to the well-being of *The Archers* as was his careful production. Any small unit working hard over long hours is bound to suffer tensions and, when you mix in the vastly different temperaments of technicians and actors, the atmosphere can often turn blue. In such situations, Tony would take an extra long drag on his cigarette while he thought of a *bon mot* that would defuse the situation.

His contribution to *The Archers* is inestimable.

When we knew that Godfrey Baseley was going, we had no doubt that his departure would leave a huge hole that would be very difficult to fill. Although I had to face this problem five times over

In control . . . producer Tony Shryane sits in front of the control desk that gives a clue to the date the picture was taken. Broadcasters who are old enough would recognise the antiquated equipment as dating from the early 1950s. Fans of The Archers could get even closer by recognising Harry Oakes and Gwen Berryman in the style of Dan and Doris circa 1955.

I spy from my little sty . . . a producer beginning with S! In the eternal search for the authentic sounds of the farmyard, Tony Shryane confronts a prize porker with a microphone that could have come out of the Ark.

the years, it never became any easier to shake off the awful feeling that the outgoing editor was irreplaceable. In Godfrey's case, however, it was true. And rather than try the impossible – to find a second Godfrey – we decided to reorganise the management structure of the programme.

My drama colleagues had told me that the current problems with the programme undoubtedly stemmed from poor scripts . . . hardly surprising when you remember that just two people had been writing them for more than 20 years. We therefore made Tony Shryane the pivotal figure . . . still as the producer but now with overall responsibility, and we began the search for a script editor who would concentrate on the writing side of the operation.

It was a critical time for the programme. An audience research report at the time said that people were 'beginning to doubt the realness and credibility of the serial, which is perhaps strengthened by the fact that many former listeners have stopped listening because they find the programme dull and the characters and storyline unreal'.

The controller of Radio 4 at the time was the late Anthony Whitby. One of the BBC's most brilliant current affairs men, Tony wasn't exactly an *Archers* fan. Luckily, however, his elderly mother was an avid listener and he was therefore never under any illusions about the programme's importance. When I said we needed to buy our way out of trouble, he didn't argue but quickly found the money that was to lure Malcolm Lynch away from *Coronation Street*.

At the time, most people thought we were daft to even think of trying to attract a man at the height of his success in the most popular programme on television. But my philosophy was: nothing ventured, nothing gained. I put my financial package together and approached Malcolm. He was clearly intrigued by the idea of reviving the fortunes of *The Archers* but he was very cautious about our offer. However, I had been acting as caretaker editor of the programme and my determination to appoint a professional turned me into a silver-tongued salesman. To my delight, after nearly two months' deliberation, Malcolm took the bait. He accepted the job of pulling *The Archers* back from the brink of disaster . . . and let me off the hook.

It is, of course, a long way from The Rover's Return to The Bull; from the grittiness of the industrial north to the ostensibly gentler shires of rural England; and from the highly technical grammar of television production to the more esoteric style of radio programme-making. And there's no denying that Malcolm's appointment confirmed many people's worst fears about the new management. But what no one knew was that because of the effective death sentence hanging over the programme, only very radical changes were likely to do the trick.

Malcolm was radical. When he arrived, he started by virtually taking the programme apart . . . looking at every aspect of the writing, from the dialogue to the content, from the characterisation right down to the length of individual scenes. It was a painful process and one of the writers said later that it was like undergoing major surgery . . . without the anaesthetic.

The end result was that the programme took on a new and sharper dramatic shape. There are some who will say it wasn't the gear change I had promised but more like pulling off a B-road and finding yourself in the middle of Silverstone motor-racing circuit. Certainly, there was a great upsurge of speed in the action. In one week alone there was a plane crash, a nasty attack on a local girl and the parish church bells came tumbling down.

It was traumatic for listeners and cast alike. Some of the listeners didn't like finding themselves in the second half of the twentieth century. Norman Painting described the experience as salutary and uncomfortable and June Spencer always refers to it as the time when she went through a change of script editor.

For my part, I sometimes wondered what I had done. An earlier boss's warning that even the slightest of changes in the programme could be accompanied by 'melodrama of monumental proportions' rang loudly in my ears. The choice between 'disaster' and 'melodrama' was little better than getting out of the frying pan and finding yourself in the fire! I wasn't very happy when the plane crash was followed by the bells coming down . . . but at least it meant they weren't there to sound a death knell.

Malcolm certainly made his mark. He did the unthinkable by changing the balance between agricultural information and drama, and suddenly the programme found a new lease of life. Unfortunately, the energy and hours he had put into the job inevitably started to take their toll on his health and, under threat of a developing heart condition, he left after just less than a year to take life easier in the south of England.

Because of Malcolm's urban background, one of the precautions we took on his arrival was to support him by asking Anthony Parkin, the BBC's very distinguished agricultural editor, to act as a special adviser to the programme and this was to stand us in good stead during the next transitional phase.

Charles Lefeaux was intended as a stop-gap editor. He had just retired from the radio drama department in London and wasn't even looking for a job when we approached him. Again I was faced with caution, this time bordering on lack of enthusiasm. It was only through the good offices and persuasive style of the head of drama that he was persuaded to give up his hard-earned leisure to take on one of the hardest of daily grinds. Just when he thought he would be spending long, happy hours walking on his beloved Hampstead Heath with his wife, Tillie, Charles found himself hurtling up and down on trains from London Euston to Birmingham New Street, with his nose seldom out of a pile of scripts.

Being a Londoner born and bred, he was somewhat nervous about taking charge of the rural idyll but that was easily resolved by Anthony Parkin's presence. Although my initial intention was that Tony should just keep a weather eye on scripts and offer the odd bit of advice, it soon became evident that he had a more important role to play. At Charles's behest, he became the agricultural soul of the programme, a role he has performed brilliantly for more than 17 years.

What Charles brought to the programme was his expertise in radio drama. As a former actor – and looking the part with an immaculate appearance topped off with a neat goatee beard – he was particularly good with the cast. In every transition, it is the actors and actresses who suffer most. They are outside the production magic circle and, therefore, don't always get to know what is going on early enough. Add to that the natural sensitivity of the artiste and the perpetual fear of not getting work and you get a great deal of nervousness. Charles understood their temperament better than anyone who had gone before and was instrumental in making me aware of the need to communicate regularly with the cast.

His experience and diplomacy allowed him to carry out another reorganisation – in which he rearranged writing schedules, restructured script conferences and brought more discipline into the studio – without creating too many waves. His greatest contribution was to restore a feeling of calmness without giving up too much of Malcolm's legacy of swift-moving plots.

In his first note to the writers, Charles effectively provided a manifesto for the second half of the seventies:

If you take my advice . . . Tony Parkin joined The Archers *in 1972 as a part-time agricultural adviser. Since then he has become a key member of the team.*

The secret and the power of all successful soap opera is that it provides the customers not only with an escape but also with characters with whom they can identify and because it is an escape they need the stability of old friends going about their business year in year out. What we need are characters, events, situations and places carefully enmeshed in a network of plausibility and reality built up over many years.

He clearly enjoyed working towards these ends because the 'stop-gap' appointment turned into one lasting more than four years.

During those four years, the writing team had seen various changes including the introduction of William Smethurst, a former journalist who had worked in the television newsroom at Pebble Mill and later in the script unit of television drama. Maybe because I had been through journalism and the newsroom too, William and I became good friends and when I had to find a replacement for Charles, he was an automatic choice. For once, I didn't have to face caution. William wanted the job and, unless my memory is playing tricks, he didn't even haggle over the salary!

He is one of those characters invariably described as mercurial. He was bursting with energy and ideas; and he had a wicked sense of humour and laughed a lot. His script meetings were always great fun. He involved the whole production team in the creation of storylines and new characters and he was able to shift the balance once more, but without causing undue alarm. Under his influence, the programme became much more of a social comedy. People were heard to laugh out loud, to make jokes and to take life a bit less seriously.

During his eight years as editor, William introduced many new characters . . . Marjorie Antrobus, Dave Barry, Mark Hebden, Kathy Perks and Nigel Pargetter, for example. He also brought back Nelson Gabriel and you can blame him for the Grundys!

Among his many talents, perhaps the most important in the long term, was his skill at achieving a rapport with the listeners. In his first note to the writers, he stressed that Radio 4 listeners were highly intelligent:

We must consider this more than we did in the past

William Smethurst joined the team as a writer and then became editor for eight years. He understood the audience and introduced more humour into the storylines.

and stop writing-down to our listeners. I think our listeners look to the programme as a dramatic expression of the established, rural, English way of life. They see in us the voice of the English shires.

If, at times, we seem to show a complacent, rather entrenched, middle-class society that enjoys itself, cares more about the harvest than world affairs, and refuses to agonise over the woes of the world or the terrors of the human condition, then that is what prosperous Midland villages are about. It is also what our listeners want to hear about.

William spotted just how strong the link was between the programme and its listeners and he set out to strengthen it. He never shirked the rogue phone calls that slipped through the protective net; he answered letters promptly and personally; he devised ingenious roadshows that allowed listeners to meet their favourite characters in places as far apart as Cardiff and Norwich, Leeds and Truro; and he wrote books . . . lots of books . . . the history of the first 30 years of the programme, an 'autobiography' of Dan Archer, a cookbook from the fair hand of Caroline Bone, two coffee-table companions and a novel set in the production office of a radio soap opera. On top of all that, he was constantly looking for new ways of marketing the programme, such as commemorative plates, miniature farmhouses and an illustrated map of Ambridge.

His restless energy wasn't always well spent, of course, and some of his ideas went a bit adrift. He was by far the most controversial of the editors and some of his storylines upset both politicians and the higher echelons of the BBC (higher up than me, that is). I have only twice had to mediate between an irate director-general and a recalcitrant member of my staff. On both occasions, the culprit was Bill. Lest this be seen as heroic, I should stress that I was more frightened of losing Bill than of the displeasure of the DG.

Then again, the profile that he achieved for the programme did not do him any harm. He started getting approaches from various radio and television companies offering much higher salaries. Despite his great commercial acumen, he resisted the lucrative offers for nearly two years. He enjoyed The Archers very much and, to his eternal credit, he never once tried to use the approaches as a lever to increase his BBC salary.

In the end, even he succumbed . . . to the lure of a free hand in revitalising Central Television's long-running soap opera, Crossroads. Lesser mortals might have baulked at the scale of such a challenge – the serial was clearly on its last legs – but Bill went into it with his eyes open.

I was sorry to see him go . . . and even sorrier when he found television jobs for two key members of our production staff, several of the writers and even a couple of actors. I couldn't blame him – he always did have an eye for talent and a readiness to reward it as best he could. Even today, I can think of no reason why he should not have shared his good fortune with those who had served him so well.

However, it didn't help his successor much. Liz Rigbey arrived to a virtually blank slate. In some circumstances, that could have been a distinct advantage but for Liz, taking on the responsibility for one of radio's flagships, it must have been something of a nightmare.

She had been with the BBC for two years when I first approached her about the job. I think the suggestion that she might switch from Farming Today, Radio 4's highly specialised early morning programme, to producing a daily soap opera came as a total surprise. She didn't see the connection at first. Nor, it must be said, did a few of my colleagues. But it was there all right. She had a strong rural and farming background, a deft touch with the pen, energy and commitment, experience of the BBC and, most importantly, the essential editorial integrity that came with that.

Liz was first appointed producer of Farming Today, alongside one of the BBC's most distinguished farming specialists, Allan Wright, who had spotted her abilities while she was working for the farming press. When Anthony Parkin decided to take early retirement, Allan became the BBC's agricultural editor . . . and promptly handed over responsibility for the popular On Your Farm to Liz.

In some ways, that could have been a poisoned chalice because Tony Parkin had created and presented On Your Farm for more than 20 years and had built up a huge personal following. Replacing him was never going to be easy. To replace him with 'a young slip of a girl', as one gnarled old farmer described Liz, seemed adventurous to say the least. It didn't take long before it became obvious that Allan had known what he was doing. Liz rose to the challenge, shrugged off a handful of male chauvinistic complaints, reshaped the programme in her own style and quickly won the approval of the audience. Against that background, I had no doubts about her talent and I was convinced that, with a short conversion course, we could soon make her into The Archers editor.

What more could we ask for?

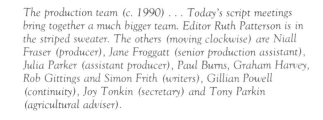

The production team (c. 1990) . . . Today's script meetings bring together a much bigger team. Editor Ruth Patterson is in the striped sweater. The others (moving clockwise) are Niall Fraser (producer), Jane Froggatt (senior production assistant), Julia Parker (assistant producer), Paul Burns, Graham Harvey, Rob Gittings and Simon Frith (writers), Gillian Powell (continuity), Joy Tonkin (secretary) and Tony Parkin (agricultural adviser).

Liz Rigbey was editor for just over two years but she livened up the programme and added an astonishing two million new listeners.

I was wrong . . . she didn't need the course! I have never seen anyone adapt to a new job as quickly as Liz. Her appetite for hard work was voracious and my own long hours paled into insignificance alongside her working day. She was in the office before anyone else arrived and she was there long after everyone had gone. She was absorbing past storylines and getting up to speed with all the complexities of running a daily serial. Within weeks it was difficult to believe she'd had no previous experience of drama production.

She quickly overcame the problems of the exodus in William Smethurst's wake, assembled her own team and got on with the job of revitalising the programme. This she did with striking success despite a catalogue of disasters that would have laid low all but the toughest of competitors.

When *The Archers* won the prestigious Sony Gold Award, BBC Radio's Managing Director, David Hatch, gave a lunch at Broadcasting House for the cast and production team to mark the achievement. Within days, six of the guests went down with hepatitis . . . four actors, the assistant producer and Liz!

Significantly, Liz was the last to show the debilitating symptoms of the virus and, with the help of the senior drama producer, Vanessa Whitburn, she was able to rearrange recording sessions and script rewrites needed to accommodate the sick actors, before finally succumbing herself.

As if that wasn't bad enough, she also had to face the deaths of several members of the cast (two of them in particularly tragic circumstances), the moving on of two assistant producers, the absence on maternity leave of the programme assistant and the resignation of a secretary. It was a very difficult time for Liz, made even more traumatic by the serious illness of her father, and eventually even she had to give in. She agreed to take six months' sabbatical leave so that she could recharge her batteries and spend more time with her parents. Sadly, her father died during that time and she simply decided that enough was enough.

We accepted her resignation with sadness. She had done a remarkable job in livening up the programme and her immediate reward was an astonishing increase of something like two million in the regular listening figures. I have no doubt that time will show she has made a lasting impression on *The Archers*.

During Liz Rigbey's sabbatical, the gap was filled first by Adrian Mourby, a drama producer from BBC Wales, and later by John Scotney, a former head of BBC Television's drama script unit and a vastly experienced radio drama producer.

Trying to keep a long-running serial ticking over is extremely difficult. The natural dynamics demand constant movement and change in both storyline and development of characters and this leaves the caretaker with a dilemma. If he doesn't press on with new ideas, the programme begins to sag alarmingly quickly. At the same time, if he institutes too much change he is seen as a bit of a

menace, who needs to be constantly watched. Both Adrian and John managed to walk the tightrope without falling off and the programme stayed firmly on course during their time.

After them came the present editor, Ruth Patterson; at 28, the youngest ever. She is evidence of the enormous talent that exists within the BBC. Like Liz Rigbey before her, she was working elsewhere in the Corporation when the vacancy occurred. It's true that she had worked briefly in the *Archers* office during her training period and for a year she'd been a director with BBC TV's *Countryfile* (the Sunday lunchtime programme), but her background was in the general features area of radio.

I was confident she was right for the job when I appointed her but even I couldn't have expected her to show so much strength so quickly. Like Liz Rigbey, she came, she saw and she conquered . . . in double quick time. I have heard nothing but admiration for the way in which she coped with the delicate situation created by someone so young moving into a key job; showed generosity towards the acting editor from whom she took over; unruffled ruffled feathers in the production office and brought out the best in the staff; eased a new girl into the difficult role of continuity assistant; treated the advisers and the writers with skill; and charmed the cast out of their understandable worries about change.

It should also be remembered that Ruth took over just before the celebrations marking the ten thousandth episode, at a time when the programme's profile was at its highest. She was under constant siege by the press and she handled every interview like a veteran. Since then, she has also shown William Smethurst's skill in promoting the programme and dealing with listeners' enquiries.

She is in the best traditions of *Archers* editors. The programme could not be in better hands . . . and confirmation of that comes from no less a source than the originator of the programme. After his first visit to the studio for many years, during which he watched her in action, Godfrey Baseley commented: 'I feel sure you have a winner in her . . . we found we had much in common about the basic principles of the programme. I hope she will stay with the programme for a long time to come.'

— CHAPTER FIVE —

THE WRITERS

Unless you've been mocked by a blank sheet of paper, an immobile typewriter or an unhelpful pencil, it's very difficult to understand fully the anguish that can beset writers. For those with deadlines, the problem can be ten times worse. For scriptwriters under the kind of pressures that a daily soap opera creates, the creative process can easily turn to hell.

I have seen dozens of *The Archers* scriptwriters at close quarters and witnessed a great deal of the angst over these past 20 years. I have watched grown men cringe before the blankness, watched pencils being sharpened over and over again and arranged into unnecessarily neat rows. I've seen gallons of tea and coffee consumed while someone waited for the muse. I've shared the joy of the telephone ringing to drag the victim away from the typewriter for a few moments' blessed relief . . . and I've listened to the excuses for words failing to come at the crucial moment. Indeed, if anyone could offer an excuse for not writing that I haven't already come across, I'd willingly pay good money for it!

Against that background, I can only marvel at the tenacity of the early writers. Imagine the endurance of Geoffrey Webb who, over 11 years, wrote half the programme's scripts . . . and think of the superhuman achievements of Edward J. Mason who wrote the other half for more than 20 years. Geoff Webb wrote nearly 1500 scripts and Ted Mason's name is on no fewer than 2700. Because of

the different way of working today, and the size of the modern writing team, neither feat can ever be matched.

These were the two men who worked with Godfrey Baseley in shaping the characters who were to become household names. Uniquely at that time but now the norm for most serials, the writers amassed dossiers on Dan, Doris, Jack, Phil and Christine and everyone else in Ambridge so that they knew them intimately before they ever put pen to paper for the first script.

One can only assume that their energy came from the excitement of this creativity. *The Archers* was their baby. They nurtured it from conception and were the midwives at the birth. They nursed it through the early, difficult days and watched with pride as it developed into a healthy toddler.

In some ways they were an odd couple. Ted Mason, a city man, was a Fellow of the Institute of Chartered Secretaries and his early career had been spent working for Cadbury's of Bournville in his native Birmingham. Geoff Webb, a countryman and a gentle giant (6 foot 4 and weighing 16 stone), had started his working life as a cub reporter on a West Country newspaper.

Although he rose to be Cadbury's Marketing Secretary, Ted Mason's real interest had always been in the world of entertainment, and he spent much of his spare time writing material for the entertaining he did at social functions. His big break came in 1936, when Stanley Holloway bought one of his monologues. The BBC, quick to spot his talent, immediately accepted his first revue scripts.

The man who recognised Ted's writing skills was the old Midland Region's variety producer, Martyn C. Webster, who was later to bring Ted and Geoff together to write *Dick Barton*. Before then, Ted showed workaholic tendencies by writing books and lyrics for a large number of half-hour radio revues and material for *Children's Hour*.

Soon after war was declared, he joined the Royal Army Service Corps and within 12 months he was promoted to sergeant. He landed in Normandy with the Allied invasion forces and went on with them to Berlin.

Back in Civvy Street, he was soon as prolific as before. In between *Dick Barton* scripts, he created *Mrs Dangerfield*, the lady detective; and in 1949, he wrote another serial, *The Lady Craved Excitement*. Then came *Meet Christopher Blaze* (starring Jack Hulbert), *Danger Money*, *The Devil to Pay* and *Missing, Believed Murdered*.

He began work on *The Archers* in 1950. And although he was in at the beginning, he always claimed he found it very difficult to create the illusion of naturalness that Godfrey Baseley demanded of the scripts. 'Writing dialogue like that needs almost *Brains Trust* brilliance,' he said.

He never quite understood the runaway success of *The Archers*: 'It has always been a source of wonder to many, myself included, that ordinary people should be happy to turn on their radio sets at the same time every day to listen to the adventures of ordinary people.'

Geoffrey Webb was 31 when *The Archers* began. Like Ted, his early job was simply a precursor to his broadcasting career. During his time as a reporter, he freelanced in his spare time and collaborated with a friend in writing plays.

His wartime service was with the RAF, where he was posted to Command Intelligence to do radio, film and public relations work. He spent three years around the Mediterranean and on the Continent and, while in Africa and Italy, he was attached to British Forces Radio, writing news commentaries, magazine programmes, variety shows and plays.

At the end of the war, he stayed with the

The loneliness of the long-distance writer . . . Edward J. Mason was one of only two scriptwriters for more than 20 years. With Geoffrey Webb and Godfrey Baseley, Ted created the original characters and went on to produce more than 2700 scripts.

British Forces Network and worked in Hamburg as a writer and producer . . . doing six different shows a week, ranging from drama and features to large-scale variety.

He left at the end of 1946, to join up with Ted Mason to write the *Dick Barton* scripts. In 1947, he spent weeks with a travelling circus to get the background to write a summer serial, *The Daring Dexters*. And in his spare time, he turned out short stories, feature articles, film scripts for American television and scripts for a variety of British artistes.

It's only when you note the prodigious output of Ted Mason and Geoff Webb and the boundless energy of Godfrey Baseley that you realise just how much effort must have gone into those early days.

When Geoff Webb died – in a car accident at the age of 42 – Godfrey Baseley was quoted as saying he was almost irreplaceable. Certainly, the task facing any new writer was formidable: 'He'll have to learn the background of the characters all the way back through three generations and he'll have to understand their interests, their foibles and the way they relate to each other. That means 3029 episodes to plough through.'

I'm not sure whether or not he ever did quite that but David Turner, by then well established as a playwright (his *Semi-Detached* went to the West End), teamed up with Ted Mason. Then it was decided that a third writer was necessary as a kind of insurance policy, and the Scottish novelist, John Keir Cross, joined them.

John Keir Cross was a colourful character, who had started writing for the amateur theatre when he was still in his teens. In 1935, he'd set out

Get out of jail and go straight to Ambridge . . . John Keir Cross had a background as colourful as any his novelist's imagination could have created. He left his home in Perth to cycle to London, with only two ventriloquist's dummies as company. En route, he was arrested on suspicion of murder and spent the night in Paisley jail before the police realised they had the wrong man!

to seek fame and fortune and left Perth on his bicycle, with two ventriloquist's dolls in the saddlebag. His journey to London, which took eight months, was interrupted when he was wrongly arrested for murder and slapped in jail for 24 hours.

When John died in 1976, Norman Painting joined the team and (as is recorded in Chapter Three) went on to write nearly 1200 scripts.

The strain of writing nearly 100 episodes a year must have been tremendous. It certainly took its toll on the health of the writers and, eventually, on the programme. It is no criticism of anyone to say that some of the characters ran out of energy, some disappeared without any further mention and the odd storyline was left in the air.

Indeed, perhaps the most eloquent tribute to the early two-man writing teams is to list those who have since had a hand in the scripts: Juliet Ace, David Ashton, Tony Bagley, Michael Bartlett, Alan Bower, Paul Burns, Joan Chambers, Deborah Cook, Mona Cresswell, Diane Culverhouse, Mary Cutler, Claire Dean, Tessa Diamond, Donna Dickinson, Dave Dixon, Jane Durrant, John Fletcher, Simon Frith, Lucy Gannon, Anton Gill, Rob Gittins, Watson Gould, Graham Harvey, Peter Hayland, Brian Hayles, Susan Hill, Ginny Hole, David Hopkins, Guy Hutchins, Sam Jacobs, Terry James, Claire Jordan, Helen Leadbeater, Christopher Lee, Peter Mackie, Frances McNeil, David Marshall, Keith Miles, Anthony Parkin, James Pettifer, Margaret Phelan, Robert Pomfret, Emily Potts, Andy Rashleigh, Gillian Richmond, James Robson, Tim Rose-Price, William Smethurst, Julian Spilsbury, John Stevenson, Sue Teddern, Joanna Toye, Roger Watson, Martin Worth, Ruby Yateman.

When we increased the size of the writing team, we quickly came up against the problems of writing by committee, and had to devise more foolproof methods of maintaining continuity and stopping characters suffering dramatic personality changes between writers. Today, there are never fewer than eight writers in the team, working on a rolling basis so that no one faces too many blank sheets of paper and so that they can continue to work in other areas.

Script conferences – once extremely formal,

presided over by the head of programmes and often with network controllers present – are now much more fun. They happen once a month and while the editor always arrives with a clear pattern in mind, storylines are thrown around like hot potatoes or enthusiastically grabbed depending on the mood of the moment. Everyone, secretaries included, is expected to make a contribution.

What hasn't changed over the years, is the writers' commitment to *The Archers*. After all the good-natured badinage, they each go off to their chosen den, to lock themselves away and write, in the knowledge that 7½ million people are going to be hanging on their every word. That is a great discipline.

The current writers are Paul Burns, Mary Cutler, Simon Frith, Rob Gittins, Graham Harvey, David Hopkins, Sam Jacobs and Gillian Richmond.

The longest-serving member of the team is Mary Cutler. A former teacher who wrote in her spare time, she only submitted a trial script after hearing one written by a life-long friend, Helen Leadbeater, and feeling she could do just as well. Luckily for her, William Smethurst had just become editor and was looking for new talent. She has now been writing for *The Archers* for ten years.

She has, however, been a fan of the programme since she was very small. The death of Grace Archer, she says, shocked her to the core at the tender age of six and she recalls playing 'Phil Archer and his pigs' – with her younger brothers as the pigs!

She loves writing scripts for a programme that people are so attached to, and finds that the rich background of the characters gives her a lot to draw on. 'On bad days, it's difficult to dream up new situations for the characters to get into. Everything has been done before.' Most of the time, though, she finds it easy because: 'They're real people in Ambridge. I just dip in and out of their houses to see what they're doing.'

In addition to writing for *The Archers*, she has written a few *Crossroads* scripts and other bits for TV, she's about to do a *Theatre in Education* play and has also worked as a freelance journalist.

Paul Burns was born in Liverpool and took his first degree at the city's university before going on

to take a Master's degree in theatre studies at Lancaster. This stretch in academia was followed by various jobs ranging from a stage-doorkeeper to a part-time lecturer in 'social life skills'.

He finally joined the civil service and stayed for five years, reaching the grade of tax inspector. In between extracting money from taxpayers, he began to sell scripts; in fact he wrote his first for *The Archers* in the same week he took his inspector's exams.

In January 1989 he gave up his job to become a full-time writer and that, he says, is much better than inspecting tax forms. He enjoys writing for *The Archers* because being part of a team is preferable to being on his own, with only a word-processor for company.

While Paul finds writing about the characters quite easy – 'Fifteen years as a listener has made me feel I know them inside out' – he doesn't like the deadlines – 'If it's going badly, it can be pretty awful.' He has now written for all the characters and says, 'I went off Shula when she married Mark instead of Neil and Caroline Bone is definitely my ideal woman!'

Simon Frith has spent much of his life living in Ambridge-like countryside in Gloucestershire. He was educated at the local grammar school, read philosophy at York University and fine art at Bristol. Before becoming a full-time writer, he trained as a sculptor and worked as a photographer. Then he worked as a carpenter and spent two years as a part-time shepherd!

He wrote his first script for *The Archers* in 1983 and he recalls his first meeting with the cast: 'It was traumatic putting faces to voices that were part of my childhood.' He thinks his scripts reflect his way of life but that doesn't make the job any easier: 'Writing scripts is as difficult as it ever was... but very satisfying at the same time.'

Of all the characters, he was most fond of Walter Gabriel, and had the sad but memorable task of writing the scene in which Walter was found dead.

In addition to his work on *The Archers* he writes other radio scripts and plays and is currently working on a novel.

Rob Gittins, a Mancunian, has never had to

work to finance his hobby – he's always been a professional writer. His first radio play was accepted in 1979 and since then he's written 15 more plays, scripts for radio and television (including *EastEnders*) and has also written two books, one of which was based on the award-winning documentary he wrote on the last week of Dylan Thomas's life in New York.

He's been writing with the team for about three years and describes his technique as being 'sit and do!' He found his first year the trickiest: 'Trying to fit the storyline together is a bit like doing a jigsaw puzzle.'

The Archers writing system suits him because it gives the writers a say in the storyline and means he usually ends up with a set of stories he likes. His Ambridge favourites are Elizabeth, Nelson and Nigel because they're quirky characters with different speech patterns and rhythms. 'And, of course, they're fun to write about.'

Graham Harvey's background is firmly entrenched in agriculture. He took a degree in the subject at Bangor; then, after a few more years' research, he spent a year on a farm in Devon, working as a stockman. In 1972, he put his agricultural experience and his writing aspirations together and became a trainee reporter with *Farmer's Weekly*.

He still freelances, mostly for newspapers and magazines, but says he will write for anything he's interested in – especially *The Archers*, which he joined five years ago. He'd been a keen listener for 20 years before he decided to submit a trial script. William Smethurst accepted it and, since then, Graham has found his specialised knowledge extremely useful.

He gave the programme something of a scoop when he introduced the subject of BST (Bovine Somatotrophin), the growth hormone used to stimulate milk production in cows. He was the first journalist to write about BST in the UK and although *The Archers* wasn't responsible for making it a national issue, he feels it certainly played a part in opening the debate.

His favourite characters, the Grundys and the farming side of the Archer family, are testament to his leaning towards agriculture. He also likes Lynda Snell though he doesn't really sympathise with her.

David Hopkins was born in Ireland but the family moved to London when he was only six weeks old. His early plans were to become an actor and he went to the Guildhall School of Music and Drama. The thought of writing didn't cross his mind until he was out of work as an actor. He had to face 190 rejections before he actually sold a script but then, that was it! He has since written 150 television scripts and about 140 radio scripts.

He too had always listened to *The Archers* – 'mainly because it was on at lunchtime' – but he only thought about writing for it when he moved out of London to North Shropshire. He lives in the village of Gobowen, in a farming area, and 'it just seemed appropriate'.

He first wrote two weeks' scripts for Liz Rigbey but then got involved with other work and only rejoined the team when Ruth Patterson became editor. He describes the experience as being 'great fun but quite the most complicated thing when it comes to the logistics of scripts and casting.'

Sam Jacobs went to school in Birmingham and first started listening to *The Archers* after being furious that *Dick Barton* had been taken off the air.

In 1959, his aspirations as a designer were thwarted when he was thrown out of Birmingham Art School. But perseverance paid off and, eight years later, he was accepted at the Central School of Theatre Design in London, where he trained under Ralph Kotai.

It was only after 15 years of theatre and television designing that he felt a change of direction was needed and he became a writer.

His first two plays were rejected, then the BBC bought the third. He worked with Piers Plowright, director of *Waggoner's Walk* at the time, who recommended him to Liz Rigbey in 1986.

With more than three years' experience under his belt, he now tends to begin writing in the afternoon, after the lunchtime episode. Although people assume *The Archers* is written tongue-in-cheek, Sam finds he can only write about the characters with great affection. He does, however, accept that a certain madness creeps in after working on the programme for a while and was sure he saw Mark and Shula at Wimbledon one year!

He also feels that 'Mrs P. and Mrs A. should be

made Dames of the British Empire as they represent the best and the worst in the British!' Mrs P. in particular holds a special place in his affections and he writes about her 'as if she were my Kentish grandmother!'

Sam had the privilege of breaking Jean-Paul's silence, with his first spoken words at Jennifer's venison dinner party. He was also given the task of writing David's proposal to Ruth and then planning the wedding.

Beyond Ambridge, he has written three television plays, four stage plays, eight radio plays and several documentaries for Piers Plowright, now one of radio's most distinguished producers.

Gillian Richmond read economics and politics at Durham University but had always intended to be a writer. Initially, she had to finance the bug by taking various other jobs including acting in Wales, being a publicist for a theatre company in Devon and a primary school teacher in London. She started writing for the programme in December 1986.

For her, The Archers has simply always been there – 'I've just dipped in and out of it' – and she writes about the characters as if they were friends. 'From a professional point of view,' she says, 'a major satisfaction is getting a chance to develop and find out about characters over a long period of time. The characters are wonderfully rich.' Her philosophy on life is that the world must be all right as long as The Archers is still on!

She is, however, primarily a stage writer and her credits include In The Groove (her first play, performed in 1984 by the Bubble Theatre), Ellen (1985), The Last Waltz (1986/88/89) at Greenwich, and Sitting Duck at The Wolsey Theatre in Ipswich.

In 1988, she won a Thames Television bursary and became the writer-in-residence at the Soho Poly Theatre in London. She recently finished another play, The Legacy, and also finds time to write for television, including EastEnders.

Difficult as the task of the writers is, at least on The Archers they are supported by excellent specialist advisers. First and foremost among them is undoubtedly Anthony Parkin, our agricultural adviser.

He joined The Archers in 1972, when he was asked to give agricultural advice to the new editor, Malcolm Lynch (newly arrived from Coronation Street and with no rural experience). It was a loose, part-time arrangement that was expected to last a few months, but Tony has now been a key member of the production team for more than 17 years. Although the original intention was that he should simply keep a weather eye on the scripts and offer occasional advice, he soon became the agricultural soul of the programme.

His background meant that he was ideally suited to the job. He was born and brought up in the country, and on leaving school he spent four years working on a farm in Kent. After wartime service in the RAF and three years at Reading University, he became an agricultural journalist. He joined the BBC in 1960 and later created the ever-popular radio programme On Your Farm. He combined that with running a small farm in Worcestershire and was then appointed as the BBC's agricultural editor.

Since joining The Archers, Tony has been an invaluable source of information and advice to five editors and a long list of writers. He created profiles for every farm in Ambridge and developed an annual farming calendar that keeps writers up to date with what should be going on throughout the changing seasons. He has also shown the writers that he understands their problems by joining the scriptwriting rota from time to time.

The value of his contribution to the programme was underlined in September 1989, with the publication of The Archers Book of Farming and the Countryside, in which he provides a fascinating background to the farming and rural life of Ambridge.

The programme also has the benefit of other regular advisers. For many years Phil Drabble provided country notes, of particular value when Tom Forrest introduced the Sunday-morning omnibus edition. Currently, the other advisers are Dr Fiona Kameen (general medicine), John Pogmore (gynaecology), the Reverend Jeremy Martineau (religion) and Edward Allsop (land management).

— CHAPTER SIX —

IN THE MIDST OF LIFE . . .

AMONG THE MOST DIFFICULT problems for any long-running programme is the natural process of growing old and the inevitability of death. *The Archers*, which has now been going for close on 40 years, has suffered more than its fair share of traumas, both within the programme and among the writers and cast.

On the air, the most dramatic death (perhaps the most dramatic on any radio or television programme before or since) was, of course, that of the young Grace Archer. Although it happened more than 30 years ago, it is talked about even now in hushed tones and still arouses vivid memories along the lines of where-were-you-the-night-Grace-died?

In those early days, the very idea of a storyline in which someone central to the plot should actually die was taking realism too far for most people. For example, in 1953, when June Spencer wanted to leave the programme to start a family of her own, the possibility of killing off Peggy Archer (then a young mother of three) was contemplated . . . but not for long. The matter had to be referred to the highest echelons of the BBC and, very swiftly, the message came back: 'We [the Controller of the Light Programme and the Director of the Home Service] both feel that to have a death in *The Archers* would be a most unfortunate thing and I hope you will therefore be able to resolve your difficulty, if necessary, by employing another actress.'

Two years later, when the tricky subject was raised again, there had been a clear change of policy; either the British public had become a tougher breed or the BBC bosses had lost their scruples. The outcry that arose after Grace Archer's death in the stables fire at Grey Gables suggests that it was the BBC that had changed. The listeners were definitely not ready for such a shock.

What brought about the change was, clearly, the threat of competition from the new commercial television channel. In June 1955, the writers and production team met for the regular monthly script conference at the BBC headquarters in Birmingham. The routine business was dealt with in brisk and efficient fashion but when the subject of commercial television was introduced, the whole nature of the meeting changed.

Everyone was sworn to secrecy – hardly surprising with death on the agenda! And the secretary, Valerie Hodgetts (later to marry producer Tony Shryane), was told not to duplicate and distribute minutes as she had always done up to then.

The meeting unanimously agreed that of all the dramatic options, the death of a major character would have the greatest impact. Next, came a discussion about who should be the victim and a shortlist was drawn up – Christine Archer, Carol Grey (later to become Mrs Tregorran) and the newly-wed Grace Archer. It is not clear who voted for whom, but in the end it was Grace who was chosen to be the sacrificial lamb.

Then came what must have been a fairly cold-blooded discussion in which someone pointed out that, because of her independent nature, Grace was not one of the best-loved characters. After her marriage to Philip Archer, she had upset him and, therefore, many of the audience by declaring she had no intention of starting a family. In an effort to increase her popularity and consequently make her death more shocking, it was agreed that Grace should change her mind, become pregnant (this was actually in the script just two weeks before the death) and thus endear herself to all the listeners.

Having thus hatched the plot, the mood of the meeting seemed to change again and the ensuing comments showed commendable concern for the audience.

Grace should die after a miscarriage, said someone. No, no, that would upset every expectant mother in the land.

Grace should die in a road accident. No, that would frighten everybody whose wife was out in her car at the time.

How about her dying in a stable fire, then? Yes, that was it – and if she first escaped the flames then rushed back into the blazing stable to try to save her horse, would not that be a fitting end for a heroine?

With the conspiracy concluded, the problem then became one of security. Any leak and the whole plan would collapse. As well as not circulating the minutes, no further discussion was to take place until the day of the event. By way of camouflage, it was agreed that during the appropriate week an experiment on topicality would be conducted. This meant that instead of writing the scripts in advance, Ted Mason and Geoffrey Webb would try doing it on the day of the broadcast so that they could work in as many up-to-date references as possible. For good measure, it was also decided that the episode should be recorded in London.

It all worked like a charm. Outside those at the meeting, no one guessed that anything was afoot. The cast, who usually had their scripts the previous week, were quite happy with the story Tony Shryane spun them about the topical try-out.

On the day itself, the BBC publicity office was told – in one of the great understatements in broadcasting history – that The Archers that evening

would be 'quite interesting' and it might be a good idea to invite the press in for a preview. This was done, and such was the popularity of the programme at the time (one in three of the adult population listened every day) that all the national daily papers were represented at about five o'clock, deliberately too late for that day's evening papers, when the episode was recorded.

As the final scene ended, with Phil saying, 'She's dead!' there was a stunned silence. The tough, hardbitten newsmen didn't quite believe what they'd just heard. Perhaps because there was no closing signature tune, they assumed there had been some kind of mix-up. They sat around uncertainly. They had never faced death quite like this before.

Then all hell broke loose, with reporters dashing everywhere, trying to speak to the cast, the writers, the producer and the editor all at the same time. In the confusion, one young journalist, who'd obviously seen too many films about his trade, snatched the nearest telephone and dialled his office to tell them about the scoop, only to discover that it was a dummy phone used as a studio prop.

In the end, he and all the others found real telephones and told their stories, but not before the listeners had heard it themselves that evening.

In the days that followed, the BBC estimated that they received some 15 000 letters of protest – it was impossible to count the number of phone calls. For fear they would be inundated with flowers, it was decided that the 'funeral' would not be held within the programme.

While the front-page headlines recorded the shock waves that spread throughout the country, the actress who played Grace, Ysanne Churchman, could barely hide her own sorrow. Her comment was short but hugely expressive: 'I am sorry so many people are miserable about the death of Grace Archer. It was no wish of mine. I have enjoyed playing the part.'

Clearly, the impact was greater than anyone associated with the programme could have imagined and its effect was dramatic. It was more than 15 years before another member of the Archer family was killed off. There were other deaths, notably Janet Tregorran (John's first wife) killed instantly in

The generation game . . . Dan Archer always found time to be helpful and while his son Phil sometimes thought he knew better, grandson Tony was always much more appreciative of his advice.

a car accident, but they didn't have the same sort of impact.

In the intervening years, some key members of the cast died, including the original Dan Archer (Harry Oakes) in 1960, and the man who replaced him (Monte Crick) in 1969. In each case they were replaced by other actors.

Two writers also died during this period. In June 1962, Geoffrey Webb, one of the original writers, was killed in a car crash. And five years later, in January 1967, John Keir Cross, the man who replaced him, died after a long illness. In each case, they died in harness – writing scripts only days before their death – and the effect on the programme was as professionally debilitating as it was personally saddening. The other writer, Edward J. Mason, and the production team weren't allowed a decent grieving period. The pressure of producing additional scripts and looking for a replacement was simply too great.

When Ted Mason died in early 1971, Norman Painting described it as one of the most serious body-blows of the programme's history. It was Ted – working with Geoffrey Webb, to Godfrey Baseley's grand design – who had created the original characters . . . Dan and Doris, Jack and Peggy, Phil and Christine and all the other villagers of Ambridge.

He had written more than 2700 scripts – a record that can never be equalled – and had sustained the programme through the deaths of his two colleagues, writing all the scripts singlehandedly for long periods. He was the repository of 20 years of folklore. No one knew the twists and turns of the storylines or the quirks and peculiarities of the characters like he did. Edward J. Mason was, in fact, irreplaceable. What was to come after him was a whole new system of writing teams.

It was perhaps because Ted was no longer around to sound a cautionary note that, later in 1971 (a year after I had taken on executive responsibility for *The Archers*), the producers felt able to deal with another family death . . . and even then we fudged it for quite a long time.

Our difficulties were caused by the death of Denis Folwell, the actor who had played Jack Archer since the beginning. Unknown to me, the editor and two scriptwriters met and decided on a storyline in which Peggy would find Jack slumped in his chair, apparently asleep. Only slowly would she realise that he had quietly passed away. Norman Painting, then one of the writers, said later: 'We felt that the character should not be re-cast and if carefully written, the death scene would offend no one.'

While I agreed we should not try to replace Denis, I was uncertain about the alternative. My feelings were confused by the fact that our twenty-first anniversary was coming up within weeks. We were planning extensive celebrations and I argued that, for the time being, we should avoid the obvious saddening effect the death of Jack would have on the listeners.

Instead, it was decided that Jack who had been ill for some time, would go away to a sanatorium for treatment and that he would die, off-stage, some time after the anniversary. The writers explained how difficult it was to keep a major character like Jack in the plot without the listeners ever hearing him. So I compromised and agreed that we should find an actor with a similar voice to do just two short scenes to maintain the illusion.

Tony Shryane asked Edgar Harrison (then playing Dan Archer) to read some lines which Norman Painting had written for Jack. The voice match was uncanny but, as an extra precaution, Tony decided to have Jack talking to Peggy only on the telephone from the sanatorium.

I wasn't present at the recording but when the tape was played to the cast, most of them were visibly moved by the similarity in the voice. One actor, who had worked for many years with Denis Folwell, cried.

In a close group like the programme's cast and production team, the death of one of the members hits you on different levels – personally and professionally – but the separate reactions merge with bewildering speed into a single emotion . . . despair. Tony Shryane, producer for 28 years, described it graphically in an article he wrote for the BBC internal newspaper, *Ariel*, soon after the death of Gwenda Wilson, who played Aunt Laura.

When Denis Folwell died, his character, Jack Archer, was kept alive in the script until after the programme's twenty-first anniversary celebration. Denis is seen here with Thelma Rogers, who played Peggy for a short while.

Gwenda and I had been friends for many years, even before she joined the programme 20-odd years ago. She was a delightful artiste whose infectious gaiety made her popular with everyone and she had that indefinable Australian quality that kept her going at parties when everyone else was beginning to fade. When she died, I could not believe that her energy and enthusiasm would no longer be there to enliven the recordings. But then – and this is where, I think, the real sadness comes in – I had to abandon my personal feelings and decide what to do about the programme and the recordings already made with Gwenda. It may seem like an easy decision . . . the show must go on is part of our folklore; and somewhere in one's head there's 'Gwenda would want it that way!' Would she? Or is that rationalisation because, in honesty, it is also the easiest way out?

Finally, you do make the decision and the recordings do go out. Her voice comes up . . . as Aunt Laura, the crotchety old busybody of Ambridge. What have you done? That's not how you want Gwenda to be remembered.

Then . . . and perhaps again it's rationalisation . . . you realise you're straying from the narrow line between soap-opera fiction and real-life fact. Gwenda was an actress and that was another of her wonderful performances. That **is** how she would want to be remembered. The first big emotional hurdle is over.

Back in the studio, the actors and actresses are having their own problems in coping. The company is almost as tightly knit as many families and the need to talk and talk about Gwenda conflicts with the need to rehearse the next episodes.

The first time Aunt Laura is mentioned in the script, the atmosphere threatens to become unbearable. Then the red recording light goes on and everyone goes into professional overdrive. Personal feelings are kept at bay . . . at least for a while. Our next problem is to decide what to do in the long term about the character in the storyline and, yet again, personal feelings clash uncomfortably with professional instincts. Do we re-cast or do we rewrite Aunt Laura out of Ambridge?

Re-casting will not be easy. Gwenda created Aunt Laura and had developed the character in her unique style over 20 years and more. To find someone else to take on the role and carry it off as Gwenda did seems, at the moment, to be trying for the impossible. At the same time, the very strength of Gwenda's characterisation had made Aunt Laura one of the key personalities of Ambridge, an indomitable lady seldom far from centre stage. She is one of the village's doers . . . and that makes her a tremendous asset to the scriptwriters.

What will we do? I don't know yet. All I do know, is that we are in for many long hours of agonising discussions. Sadly it has all happened before – the last time only a few months ago when Julia Mark (who played Nora McAuley) died – but it doesn't get any easier.

Tony was right. When, in 1980, it was decided that Doris Archer, the family's 80-year-old matriarch, should die – 'quietly at her home, Glebe Cottage, Ambridge, on October 26' – the discussions were no less protracted and the angst was, perhaps, even greater.

The decision that Doris should die was forced on us by a promise I had made some years earlier to the late Gwen Berryman, when she had come close to retiring because of painful and crippling arthritis. Sometimes the pain made Gwen very depressed and, on one such occasion, she told me the only reason she kept going was because she was frightened of what we would do with the part if she left.

She explained that she felt she had put so much of herself into the part of Doris that she wouldn't be able to cope if someone else took on the role. By way of reassuring her, I promised that if and when she did eventually retire, we would not re-cast.

When Gwen suffered a stroke at the age of 75, it left her partially paralysed and impaired her speech. It was soon evident that she was unlikely to rejoin the cast. Personal concern for her far outweighed professional considerations and as we waited for the shock of her illness to ebb away, we did nothing but ease Doris quietly into the background.

However, after several months, the writers were having increasing difficulty coping with an off-stage Doris and it became obvious that we would either have to break my promise to Gwen and find a new actress or write the character out permanently. After much heart-searching, it was decided Doris should die.

When I went to break the news to Gwen, I found her in remarkably good spirits and with her speech enormously improved. She told me she was feeling great and looking forward to returning to work. I was so surprised that I backed out of telling her what we had done – the death scene had already been recorded – and made a hurried telephone call to the studio to arrange a postponement.

However, the next day, Gwen's brother rang me to say that I had seen her in a very rare moment of well-being. The reality was gloomy and her doctor confirmed that she would never be able to go back to work.

The death scene went ahead as originally planned. Gwen didn't hear the programme but she was told about it later and took it remarkably well. At least she knew that no one else would play Doris Archer.

Around the time of Doris Archer's death, Philip Garston-Jones, the actor who created the character of Jack Woolley, had the grim experience of reading his own obituary notices. Staying at a Birmingham hotel between recording sessions, Philip had a heart attack and was rushed into hospital. Another member of the cast, also staying in the hotel, heard about the incident but thought Philip had died. He telephoned Pebble Mill and very quickly it became official and a note was released to the press.

Consummate showman that he was, Philip took it all in good part and laughed uproariously. 'Now that I know what you all think of me, I can afford to go,' he told me. He died a short time later.

The sadness of death and the strains it can cause in a small, tight-knit group were underlined when Haydn Jones, the actor who created the Joe Grundy character, died suddenly in 1985. Haydn was one of the most popular members of the cast and the shock of his death left everyone deeply upset. Matters weren't helped when it transpired that his funeral was to take place on one of the predetermined recording days.

Fixing the recording schedule is one of the nightmares of the programme's production staff because it means trying to match the availability of actors with the wishes of the writers. On this occasion, William Smethurst was faced with the impossible task of balancing the urgent needs of the schedule with the natural wishes of the cast to be at the funeral.

In the end, he decided that, as in the old maxim, the show must go on and he reluctantly pressed on with the recording. The programme, he said, would be represented at the funeral by those members of the cast and production team not involved in the recording.

Unfortunately, one of those booked to be in the studio was Heather Bell, who played Joe Grundy's daughter, Clarrie. She and Haydn had been very close and she very much wanted to

The one and only . . . Gwen Berryman played Doris Archer for more than 30 years. Her long service with the programme won her an MBE and the promise that the part would never be re-cast when she eventually retired.

attend the funeral. She was particularly upset and made a special plea to be excused from the recording. Because that would have affected other members of the cast and would also have meant considerable rewriting of the script, William said it wasn't possible.

Heather's grief turned to anger and, sadly, she resigned amid a great deal of acrimony. The atmosphere in the studio was decidedly uncomfortable for many months afterwards.

Natural deaths and accidents are hard enough to cope with, but within the space of a year *The Archers* team had to come to terms with the suicide of two of the cast. Fiona Mathieson, the girl who replaced Heather Bell as Clarrie Grundy, was found dead in an Inverness hotel. She had taken an overdose. Ted Moult, who'd only joined the cast as a bit of fun, was discovered in the office of his Derbyshire farm. He had shot himself.

The shock of these events is indescribable. I cannot say how other members of the team coped. We were unable to speak about it, so terrible was the trauma. Even today, I find I can do little more than reproduce the obituary I wrote at the time for the *Daily Telegraph*.

Welcoming Ted Moult as he walked through the door was a bit like letting in a great gust of fresh air that had just wafted over a field of new-mown grass. His personality was essentially rural – a natural wit vying with common sense so that no one could be under any illusion about where his feet were firmly placed.

He was a patently nice man who enjoyed nothing more than sharing his own pleasures with others and if his sense of humour made you laugh, so much the better. He never quite understood his popularity and he was genuinely puzzled that he could entertain an audience by 'doing nowt' as he always put it.

Perhaps that was his secret. He really didn't ever try to be funny and there was never anything studied about his witticisms, whether they came tumbling out with boyish glee on programmes like **Play School** *or in the oratorical style of* **Any Questions?**

My own enduring memories of Ted will be his appearances on grand occasions. He was a tireless worker for charitable causes – through his beloved Lords Taverners and the Stars Organisation for Spastics – and he would go anywhere to raise money. Inevitably that took him among the well-heeled and their glittering candelabras in the great banqueting halls around the country. For such occasions, he would squeeze himself into a dinner jacket and his wife, Maria, would swear that he even combed his hair: but when he arrived you always felt that he had come grinning from the back of the haycart.

That is how the people loved him: fresh down from the farm. They would hang on his every word and roar with laughter as he cheerfully and systematically stripped them of their spare cash. They enjoyed it nearly as much as Ted – but it was Ted who laughed all the way to the bank.

There was, of course, a serious side to Ted Moult. His family and his farm in Derbyshire provided the anchor, and it was from his farming interests and concerns that he derived most of his intellectual satisfaction. He enjoyed keeping up to date with agricultural politics and developments and many a politician has suffered by not recognising the sharp mind behind the hangdog drollery. In the circles where it mattered most to him, he will be remembered very much as Farmer Moult. Others may remember him best for the way he so delicately dropped a feather to demonstrate the draught-proofing qualities of a particular brand of double-glazing.

Lest anyone think that sad or ironic, share the joke – for Ted simply saw that as an opportunity to extract some of the profits from 'those rich city beggars'.

As a far-from-simple countryman, Ted would feel that such an epitaph gave him the last laugh.

By way of relieving the tension, let me share a couple of listeners' letters we received after the 1988 death of Chriss Gittins, who had played Walter Gabriel for so many years. They're both from very young fans and one wrote direct to Peggy Archer.

Dear Mrs Archer,

I always lisen to your program because my Mum has it on. I'm very worried because I haven't heard Walter Gabreel for a long time. My Mum

The wheel of fortune . . . it certainly was not! Walter Gabriel thought he could make a living out of repairing the locals' bikes, but they soon discovered he couldn't tell his Sturmey-Archer from his Dan Archer and took their business elsewhere.

says she thinks he's died but I don't think its true. I think Mrs Pea is hiding his trousers still. Can you go round and find out for me so I can pruve it to my Mum.

Thank you very much

The letter was signed by nine-year-old Jonathan Day. The second one came from 16-year-old Mark Crook.

*Having only recently discovered the joys of **The Archers** on Radio 4, Uncle Walter's crabbiness, cantankerous attitude and roguish tricks won me over instantly.*

I write to you to offer my condolences to all Mr Gittins family, friends and colleagues, who, I am

*very sure, will miss him and to his fans and listeners on this side, who will mourn the loss of one of Britain's great traditions. We still have the royal family, fish and chips, rainy summers . . . but we have lost dear old Walter Gabriel and I am sure that British Heritage and **The Archers** will never be the same again.*

Young Mark is, of course, quite right. Walter Gabriel will be sadly missed . . . as will all the others who have left the Ambridge scene.

CHAPTER SEVEN

THE LISTENERS STRIKE BACK

OVER THE YEARS, THE programme has received thousands of letters and most of the quality newspapers have carried extensive correspondence from listeners. The writers divide into various categories . . . the witty, the critical, the sympathetic and the inquisitive. But they all share one thing – a deep interest in all that goes on in and around Ambridge.

The line in the advertisement for a new *Archers* editor, about the seven million listeners knowing almost as much about the storyline as the writers and producers, was not just flannel. It's true . . . and we have the scars to prove it . . . in the piles of letters telling us where and how we've gone wrong. (Of course, we get even bigger bundles of congratulatory correspondence but I suspect that wouldn't make such interesting reading.)

We like to think we have a very healthy relationship with our listeners and that is perhaps because we do take note of much of what they say. And if we didn't do that of our own volition, there's always *Feedback*, the Radio 4 watchdog, to snap at our heels. *Feedback*'s presenter, Chris Dunkley, is a regular recipient of letters about *The Archers* and every now and then, he calls us to account. The last time he did so, I was the unlucky prisoner in the dock.

The charge was that we had let what had once been a rather superior drama serial sink to the level of a television soap opera.

First, three prosecution witnesses were called upon to give their evidence:

The Archers has declined in quality over the last few months. Its storyline has become increasingly far-fetched.

The pace of life which used to flow at a leisurely, realistic rate has accelerated. Events now race past with less preparation and few repercussions. The programme has become little more than plot development, enacted by stereotyped characters. The high point in my radio listening has been spoiled, leaving me with the taste of soap in my mouth.

The storylines have become more and more inept, and less and less true to life. I hope the new producer can give it a kiss of life and take us back to real, true-to-country-life situations once more.

I was left to take a deep breath and express regret:

I'm sorry that these people feel that way about it, because they are right as far as they are concerned. And this is our eternal problem in a programme as long-running as **The Archers***. Whatever we do, we are always going to upset a section of the audience.*

That response only encouraged Chris Dunkley to move up a gear or two. This is how the rest of the interview went:

DUNKLEY:

But are these changes which are perceived in those letters, are they ones which you recognise?

GALLAGHER:

I recognise some of the changes and I would like to

explain it by trying to look at the ethos of writing for a very long-running series like **The Archers**. We bring in new writers all the time, and we confront them with very well laid out characters, scenes, plots and so on. If we don't allow them to pick up these pieces and play around with them to some degree, we're going to stifle any creativity that they've got.

DUNKLEY:

Do you accept that you seem now to be affected in the tone of the series by what's happening in television soap opera?

GALLAGHER:

*Yes, I can understand that. We're not. But again, the writers are going to be affected by everything they see and experience around them, and if some of them spend too long watching **Dallas** and **Dynasty** and so on, it's inevitable that some of the techniques from those series are going to affect them.*

DUNKLEY:

Can we move on to some different and more detailed criticisms? Pamela Clowes of Drayton, who

also says **The Archers** is becoming totally unreal, that word again, 'unreal', believes that 'everyone's character has changed' and she ends her letter: 'I wonder if it's being made deliberately dreadful so as to lose its audience and then be dropped'. So first, how are the ratings doing?

GALLAGHER:

The ratings are doing extremely well. That's one of the difficult points. I could become extremely defensive and say but, but, but, we're putting on audience. We've increased by 20 per cent over two years. That's a huge increase. I don't really want to get into conflict with the listeners, because as far as they are concerned, they are totally right. All I would

Winning ways . . . Even Captain behaved himself when Radio Times winner, Amanda Cooper (second from the right), came to collect her prize . . . a weekend at Grey Gables. Sharing a sparkling moment are Stephen Morris (manager of Grafton Manor, the Bromsgrove country house hotel that doubles as Grey Gables), Amanda's friend Patricia Doggett, Jack Woolley, and former editor Liz Rigbey. The downside was that the girls had to read all three novels in The Archers Saga!

say to them is that while they're not liking something at the moment, it'll be their turn to enjoy something next week or the week after, because these are the essential ingredients of a soap opera. They're always changing and their turn will come soon.

DUNKLEY:

Let's push into that precise point a little further, because a lot of listeners have written saying that too many of the characters in **The Archers** have become dislikeable. One writer says: 'Phil has become so stupid. Kenton is totally unreal. Shula and Mark have turned into the most boring couple of the year, and Elizabeth is a spiteful bitch'. Elizabeth incidentally, I mean we get more letters saying how awful Elizabeth is than any other character. Marcel Edwards of Prestwick says: 'I dislike most of the characters from the smug self-satisfied Hebdens to the ones we are meant to love to hate'. And J. B. Stephens of Catbrook claims: 'Phil and Jill are weak and pathetic, and Elizabeth is a liar, a cheat and a scrounger and a drunk'. So how do you answer the charge that too many of the characters now are unlikeable?

GALLAGHER:

I can't answer it, because again I go back to what I said earlier. The listener is right. We **know** we're on a hiding to nothing, but for everyone who finds somebody boring, there are an awful lot of others who find them the most fascinating people on earth. I mean don't get me wrong, producing and working on a programme like **The Archers** is a very, very onerous occupation. It's very close to a sweatshop. People in that situation are going to get bored. They're going to get slap-happy, they're going to get slapdash. They're going to make mistakes. We need our listeners to understand that, and I think most of them actually do.

DUNKLEY:

Can we come finally to a letter from Porthcawl, from a Mr Douglas Davies, who says:

READER:

In recent years **The Archers** have developed some irritating ways which make them less true to life than they used to be. One which might now be on the wane is their inability to see and find each other, as follows:

'Phil!' – 'Over here, Uncle Tom!'

'Tony!' – 'In the milking shed, Pat!'
'Jill!' – 'We're in the kitchen, Mrs Antrobus!'
Having spotted the one they're looking for, they are then surprised to see someone else:
'Oh hello Elizabeth! I thought you were in Borchester!' David and Tony also seem unable to do any farm work, however light, without gasping for breath between their words in conversation. More recently, the series has been hit by an epidemic of 'Sorry?' and 'What?' indicating a complete misunderstanding of a statement. There were about 60 of these last week. I never hear people speak like this except in serials so a change to a more natural speech would be welcome.

GALLAGHER:

I think I have to throw up my hands and surrender to Mr Davies. That's a lovely letter. It's lovely and painful, because I recognise the reality of what Mr Davies is saying. If any of our scriptwriters are listening, be warned. There will be a knock on your door soon.

In the wake of the *Feedback* broadcast, there was another flurry of letters from people anxious to keep us on the straight and narrow. For example, there was one from a Manchester listener who described herself as an old lady. She said she didn't go out very much and couldn't bear to miss her nightly visit to Ambridge but was none too happy about some recent changes. She was concerned and critical:

Listening to **Feedback** this morning, there were a lot of people complaining about changes but that is inevitable over all these years. Times do change whether in the town or the country. What I don't like is the changes in the dispositions of the characters. Elizabeth Archer is a nasty little boring piece-of-work; Mrs Walker is unbelievable; Nigel is stupid and drinks far too much; but, to me, Shula and Mark are a lovely couple. They are not perfect but who is? Shula is honest, kind and bubbly. Sometimes she's a little down in the dumps but soon gets over it. Mark is just right for her even if, sometimes, he's a little serious. They really do care for each other, which doesn't make them boring, just a nice decent couple. They may be a little old-fashioned but none the worse for that, as dear old Mrs Antrobus would say.

Come on now, please let them have a baby. It would make Jill so happy and she has had her share of worries with the odd Kenton.

I know it takes a variety of people to make the village alive, like that interfering busybody, Mrs Snell, and the moaning Tony Archer. I suppose we must have them there or there would be no Ambridge and that would be unthinkable. But please let's not have too much of the horrible Elizabeth or the mysterious Kenton.

Wishing you, the writers, the characters and all the staff all the best. I hope the series goes on for ever, as dear old Jethro once said.

There really is no answer to such a delightful letter from a lifelong listener but it certainly cheered us all up in the office . . . as did her afterthought:

PS I think the acting of all the characters is great, even the ones I don't like, and don't you think it is time you gave Caroline a break? She is nice.

Another letter, postmarked from Llandrindod Wells in Wales, showed the writer had a deep affection for the English language and had got fed up with the way some of the writers (and she actually named them) tended to mangle it in their scripts:

*For over 20 years I've been a happy listener to **The Archers**, remembering how sensitively the producers treated Grace's death, with the episode fading out to silence instead of tum-te-tum. By now, I feel all the good folk of Ambridge are old friends.*

*Recently my suspension of disbelief has been stretched and has now snapped. The urban Americanism of using 'like' instead of 'as' or 'as if' jars horribly. For ages, Shula has used this (contaminated by the outsider, Mark?). Terry Barford could have picked up 'like I was a bogey man' from army service and Mrs Snell is obviously non-U so might possibly say: 'Sounds like she might need my help after all.' But surely Jennifer is too well educated to say: 'It looks like you've had a wasted journey.' Nigel's public school would never have tolerated his 'well, like you said'. Finally, Mrs Pargetter saying: 'That sounds like it could be fun' shattered my empathy with the programme. It was as if (not 'like') Shakespeare had titled his play, **Like You Like It**.*

Your storylines are marvellously convincing so please would you have a gentle word with your scriptwriters about this little point. Then at least one of your oldest and most loyal fans will be a happy listener again.

As the letter-writer said, it's clearly a case of 'must try harder' for some of the writers. I hope she doesn't get round to reading this book and assessing my use of English!

It should already be quite clear that our listeners aren't backward in coming forward with advice but the appointment of a new editor gave a gentleman in Durham an excuse to proffer some more:

*I was interested to read in the **Independent** about your new job, and think the following may interest you.*

*For a long time **The Archers** has represented everything that disgusts me most about the British and their rural fantasies. The banal, smug music sums it up only too well. I say this as someone who has spent the past 20 years in villages in Suffolk, Norfolk and now Weardale. While in Suffolk I ran a small centre for village studies, whose purpose was to counteract the conventional view of rural life. Here in Weardale, I started (without payment) a community newspaper whose aim was to give local people a voice and an insight into modern issues affecting their lives.*

*My struggle has been and still is to move rural experience into the centre of life for those who live in the country, to treat the **whole** world seriously from that perspective and to banish for ever **The Archers** gloss which helps to embalm rural life in quaint futility. Nuclear annihilation, economic greed, tourism etc should be just as real here as anywhere.*

The reality here is both more squalid, even sinister, as well as more stimulating than the wretched programme has dared admit. The sad truth is that rural life is trapped in its infantile role by middle-class fear and greed, terrified of life's depths and the housing market . . .

*Is there any chance **The Archers** can face this reality? I would gladly help.*

One wonders just how someone so irreconcilably opposed to the comparatively simple aims of the programme could help? What would his Ambridge be like? Brookfield would become Cold Comfort Farm at best and possibly Animal Farm at worst.

We think the Grundys are bad enough for any village to have to suffer. Armageddon will have to wait for some other passing soap.

The great thing about our critics, however, is that they don't feel the need to pull their punches. How about this from a woman who swears blind she has stopped listening to the programme ... as of the night before she wrote the letter, of course. She had nine points to make. The first one would have been enough:

The characters are incredibly bland, stereotyped, and shallow. The women are particularly bad. They are either saintly doormats like Jill, sturdy country lasses like Clarrie, or bitches like Elizabeth and Shula. Lynda Snell's voice and manner are so unrealistic as to make her a caricature.

After that, she got carried away:
With the exception of Nelson Gabriel, my favourite

Open all hours . . . A replica of The Bull was one of the highlights at a BBC Pebble Mill Open Day and visitors were able to take over the roles of their favourite characters. Nearly all the men opted to play Eddie Grundy . . . presumably for the free drink that went with the hat!

*person, there is **no humour** in the programme at all. What a dreary lot they are.*

*The right-wingery of the community is deeply offensive. Tony's wife is a tiny bit less deep-dyed conservative than the rest, but I would remind you that there are a lot of people to whom the term **Guardian**-reader is not a term of opprobrium.*

There is too much drinking on the programme. I think this is serious in a time when people should be made aware of how deleterious to our society is heavy drinking.

Residents of Ambridge are the most uncultivated people I've ever met. They never discuss books, music, art or even ideas. Phil has even stopped listening to the odd snatch of music on the radio.

Inhabitants of Ambridge are monsters of selfishness. There seems to be no awareness of the needs of the larger community. England is full of young people serving the community in all sorts of programmes like CSV, for example.

What about dealing with a very important problem – care of the aged? Give the loathsome Mrs Perkins Alzheimer's disease. I shall greatly enjoy seeing Tony and Jennifer and Lilian trying to avoid caring for her.

*I do **not** listen because I love to hate people. I find it uncomfortable to dislike characters, actually. Elizabeth Archer is so unpleasant as to be unbelievable. I had six kids who were notorious for their frankness, but none of them has been guilty of such persistent rudeness.*

Have you a religious adviser to help you? I doubt it. The former vicar was pathetic, this new one is very unpromising. The best touch was having the woman deacon marry David and Ruth. That I liked.

This correspondent did have some other suggestions to offer but my motto is to quit while you're ahead and I have decided to settle for her liking the woman deacon. As an antidote to that, I couldn't resist this letter from one of our youngest and most enthusiastic fans:

*I am a 13-year-old boy who is addicted to **The Archers**. I had been listening on and off since spring 1987. I only began to listen regularly around July 1988 after reading several books on the programme.*

*My parents recently announced plans to emigrate to Australia. I am looking forward to this but will I be able to tune into **The Archers**?*

*If yes, please could you tell me which radio station it is on, which days it is on, at what time and is there an Australian version of **Radio Times** where I could find **The Archers** cast list?*

Also, I am likely to miss a good month's worth of episodes so is there anyone in Australia I could write to for a review of the past episodes missed?

Sadly, we had to disappoint the lad, who then lived in Blackpool. Although *The Archers* was once one of the most popular programmes on Australian radio, our friends Down Under dropped it some years ago and, despite regular pleas from many ex-listeners, they have no plans to bring it back.

As well as the letters we receive in the office and the thousands the cast get direct, some of our correspondents get an extra kick out of seeing their comments in black and white, and the national press seem happy to oblige. Most of the quality papers carry *Archers* letters from time to time but the *Guardian* has made it one of its idiosyncrasies. Hardly a week goes by without someone venting their spleen or displaying their wit in the august columns.

In a letter to the *Guardian* in February 1989, I was taken to task for a clanger I dropped in one of the three books published as a trilogy a few months earlier. The first book was dramatised for Radio 4 by Peter Mackie and was broadcast as a 90-minute play. Dr Caroline Lynas of Bristol spotted the far-from-deliberate mistake and she chose to temper her caustic comment with wit:

Dan Archer has been dead since 1986. Does the 30 year rule really apply before the scandal in his past can be revealed?

*We all know that Dan's brother left Brookfield to start a new life in Canada after the two boys fought for Doris Forrest – but why has it been necessary in the last 15 years to change the name of Dan's brother from John to Ben? I compare a dramatisation of **To the Victor the Spoils** broadcast on Christmas Eve and **Twenty-five Years of The Archers**, a BBC book published in 1973, both from the pen of Jock Gallagher.*

I call upon Mr Gallagher to explain the need for this subterfuge. We have a right to know.

Dr Lynas put her finger very neatly on one of the major problems for a long-running serial . . . continuity. Despite the most elaborate system of index cards and cross-filing, it's all but impossible for an ever-changing production team to ensure that every fact is accurate.

In this instance, I was trapped by the haste in which I wrote the books. My researches showed that while I *had* called the brother 'John' in my 1973 book, William Smethurst had used 'Ben' in a later book and in the script. In retrospect, I should have devised a way round it but, instead, I made the assumption that no one would remember as far back as 1973 and I took the easy way out. Now, with Dr Lynas and many more listeners breathing down my neck, I had to offer some explanation. I decided on the tongue-in-cheek approach:

Sir – Dr Caroline Lynas fights dirty. In Wednesday's **Guardian** *she quotes my past indiscretions at me . . . citing the naive scribblings of a raw young recruit to the Ambridge society and denying me the protection of the 30-year rule.*

I produced (note I don't dignify my efforts beyond the factual) **Twenty-Five Years of The Archers** *when I was a much younger and certainly more innocent observer of the Borsetshire scene. During my extensive research, centred on The Bull and The Cat and Fiddle, it was reported to me that Dan Archer and his brother had engaged in fisticuffs over the hand of Doris Forrest. As a journalist, I accepted the probity of the story and saw it as my duty to print it. Although my notes of that time are now somewhat faded, the name of the brother was certainly recorded as John. My informant was a woman who claimed to be Dan Archer's sister-in-law, a rather loud-spoken lady, if I recall, who went by the name of Mrs Prudence Forrest.*

However, over the years (during which I acquired a degree of expertness in the gentle art of embroidery, which is not as wholly irrelevant as it may seem to those outside the **cognoscenti***) my acquaintance with the Archer family developed a degree of intimacy that allowed me to discover that John was called Ben by his immediate kin (something that Mrs Forrest may not have known because she did not have any personal acquaintance with Benjamin John Archer, who left this country in 1919, two years before she was born).*

It may be that I should not have presumed upon my special relationship with the Archers when I wrote **To the Victor the Spoils** *and if my use of the affectionate diminutive confused Dr Lynas, I apologise.*

Over the years, the programme has been accused of all manner of calumny: it's the farmer's mouthpiece; we don't include enough agriculture; we're anti the Farm Workers' Union; we're too sympathetic to the workers; we're too left-wing, too right-wing, too pro the SDP, too anti the SLD and

so on. In August 1989, a letter from a Ms Bartlett raised yet another complaint:

There seems to have been a reaction against feminism, which some observers claim to have noticed recently.

When the women of Ambridge wanted to protest about the possible amalgamation of schools, they went, not to Borsetshire County or Shire Hall but to Borchester Town Hall, although Borchester cannot be the education authority.

No doubt they were misled by reports of the NALGO dispute in the press (national newspapers believe that all local government are town hall workers and that all local government activity takes place in town halls). However, surely Kathy Perks should know who her employer is?

Is this episode designed to show that the Ambridge women should keep out of politics and leave it to their menfolk, who are magistrates, former district councillors or prospective county councillors?

Ms Bartlett was way off target when she suggested deliberate anti-feminism. After all, the editor, first among equals in the production team, is a woman and so, too, are several of the equals! Ironically, the offending script was written by one of the women and she was guilty of nothing more than living in a metropolitan area where the town hall is the seat of local government power. However, in *The Archers*, inaccuracy is a grievous enough offence in itself and everyone concerned again felt chastened.

Another nice togue-in-cheek letter in the same month, from Mrs Audrey Bland of Prudhoe on Tyne, highlighted a problem constantly faced by the editor:

This new realism is heady stuff. The revelation that Ruth Archer is in Prudhoe visiting her sick mum made me want to run out and look for her. I don't know the family – perhaps they live with Prue Forrest or John and Carol Tregorran?

In the meantime, as I have a daughter, Ruth (who isn't in agriculture) and a daughter not called Ruth (who is an agriculturist), perhaps I could stand in for her? Can this be a new form of one-upmanship – I live in a place mentioned in **The Archers***?*

Prue Forrest and John and Carol Tregorran are, of course, among the programme's silent characters, those often talked about but seldom heard speaking these days. We made an exception in 1989, when Prue appeared in the ten thousandth episode and that brought an immediate rash of letters to the *Guardian*. A Mr and Mrs Bowden wrote saying they must have been dreaming and that in turn provoked another reaction, from Michael Parker of Tonbridge in Kent:

No, Phillip and Noelle Bowden, you didn't dream it! Prue Forrest did speak on **The Archers** *last month.*

But I've been listening to this everyday story of Ambridge folk long enough to have heard the real Prue and I am telling you that the Prue we heard just recently was a fraud, an imposter hired for the occasion.

Thirty years ago, when Tom Forrest was courting and marrying her, she sounded more like Martha Woodford. Last month's Prue sounded more like Judi Dench!

I am still convinced that Mrs Forrest lies in pieces at the bottom of Tom Forrest's deep freeze among the frozen pheasants and most of those living in Ambridge are in on the crime.

It is highly significant that the only people she spoke to last month were a stranger to the place, Terry Wogan, and Jack Woolley who, let's face it, is not very bright. The rest was crowd noises and, I guarantee it, the rest will be silence from Prue Forrest.

I wonder if Mr Parker has inside information? Will we hear Prue Forrest again? Watch this space. Like Higgs, the Horrobins, Mr Rodway etc, Prue Forrest exists to lend more realism to the programme by giving a sense of scale to the village and the number of people who live there. The tenor of the many letters we receive about them also suggests they are now part of the programme's charm for many listeners.

There have been times when producers would have liked to cast them and give them speaking roles (and it does happen occasionally, as when Prue Forrest turned out to meet Terry Wogan in the ten thousandth episode). But the truth is that economics is an over-riding factor. The programme's budget, generous though it is by most standards, does not stretch to more than a certain number of characters each week.

From one village to another . . . The villagers of Sharrington in Norfolk invited Jill and Peggy Archer to open their new village hall and showed them traditional rural hospitality . . . breakfast in the country kitchen of Min Purser and her daughter, Jane.

Already, the editor has to juggle with the number of actors she can use in any episode against the needs of the storyline and the availability of cast members. Many people think the *Archers* actors and actresses work only for the programme. In fact, many of them are very busy and are often unavailable. That is why some characters seem to disappear at regular intervals.

David Blunkett, the MP for Sheffield Brightside, has been a long-time listener to *The Archers* but somewhere around the beginning of 1989, he became sorely disaffected. He wrote several private letters to the programme complaining that it had become a 'silly soap' and then his exasperation boiled over into print. He first wrote to the *Independent*:

I understand that from 8 May, Liz Rigbey is to be replaced by Ruth Patterson as editor of **The Archers**. *I have listened to* **The Archers** *since I was four years old and I am sad to say it is fast becoming a rather silly soap opera. Unless something can be done to restore the programme to* **The Archers** *we knew, then I think the time has come to switch it off. Is it me, or do other listeners agree?*

He later wrote again, this time to *The Times*:
The Conservative Party are capable of many things

but their candidates in Ambridge give the county council elections a whole new dimension.

A week before polling day, Brian Aldridge pulls out of the race for county hall in Borsetshire, a novelty in itself. What happens next is quite remarkable. Jack Woolley is asked by the local association to step forward and take his place – no need to meet registration deadlines, to have the necessary forms signed and accredited, or to have his name on the postal ballots and notices already dispatched! This development in **The Archers** dispenses with such technical niceties.

Or do the authors know something about future plans yet to be revealed to the rest of us?

The awful truth in this instance was that somewhere along the line we miscalculated the date of the elections. If that sounds implausible, let me explain: the BBC works in week numbers rather than simple dates; our programme week also defies ordinary calendars by running from Saturday to Friday (to coincide with when people like to buy the *Radio Times*). Thus, we listed the date of the 1989 elections as Day 6 of Week 19, rather than Thursday, 11 May. Add to that the fact that *The Archers* production office is working on no fewer than five timescales simultaneously (storylines are laid down three months in advance; scripts are written eight weeks ahead of time; recorded six weeks before transmission; edited a month beforehand; and then we listen to them on the air on the same day as everybody else) and you have a recipe for confusion.

By the time we realised we had dropped a clanger, several episodes had already been recorded and we were left with a major salvage job. Clearly, Mr Blunkett saw it as just another step in the programme's deterioration and a Northamptonshire listener was all too ready to agree:

David Blunkett is absolutely right about the lamentable state of **The Archers**. *With the exceptions of Phil, Jill, Nelson Gabriel, and the cow with BSE which launched the well-timed assault on the increasingly unbelievable Brian Aldridge, it is hard to think of many Ambridge inhabitants whose violent demise would cause anything other than national rejoicing.*

We must hope that Ruth Patterson will direct her scriptwriters to put the emphasis back on character rather than creaky plot and, above all, will give the agricultural story editor a proper job to do.

In case the editor contemplated accepting that advice and, with a rush of blood to the head, started laying off the actors and actresses who don't play the parts of Phil, Jill, Nelson and the sick cow, another listener (from Guildford) offered a contrary point of view, this time in the *Independent*:

Like David Blunkett, I have listened to **The Archers** *since I was four years old. Unlike David Blunkett, I think* **The Archers** *has reached new heights over the last few years. I have loved, laughed and cried with Ambridge in what seems to be the epitome of the serial.*

The rest of my family are ardent devotees of **Neighbours**. *Now everyone in Ramsay Street has had at least one car accident, two serious illnesses and discovered one long-lost relative. But life in Ambridge is more ordinary. Gone are the days when each episode reached a suspenseful climax which was repeated at the beginning of the next.*

Listening to **The Archers** *is like receiving a letter. Not one of those Jimmy-aged-11-has-passed-Grade-VIII Christmas letters, but a gentle, realistic and frequently humorous update on the everyday life of country folk.*

A venturous lot . . . When these Venture Scouts set up camp at Pebble Mill (as part of an initiative test), they invited the Ambridge locals to take pot luck for . . . a different sort of lunch. The brave souls were Nigel, Mrs Antrobus, Phil, Kenton, David and Ruth. Guess who did the washing up?

Those *Neighbours* seem to get everywhere. A London reader of *The Listener* was horrified when the Australians turned up in Ambridge, and posed a fascinating conundrum:

*Listening to **The Archers** recently, I noticed **Neighbours** mania has reached Ambridge. At 5.35 pm, Clarrie Grundy turned on her TV to watch Kylie and friends in Ramsay Street whilst a bit later, Mark Hebden found Shula listlessly watching the same show.*

*But what happens if Clarrie and Shula decided to tune into Radio 4 an hour and five minutes later? Would they be able to hear themselves or, more importantly, eavesdrop on the Ambridge gossip? Or does Radio 4 have transmitting difficulties in Borsetshire every time **The Archers** signature tune comes on?*

*I would like to know if this will start a trend in all our radio and television popular drama series. Will we be soon hearing the cast of **Brookside** discuss the latest plot developments of **The Archers**?*

*But more importantly, this could have serious ramifications down at **Coronation Street** and **EastEnders**. If either of these two soaps are supposed to reflect real life, then most of the cast should be sitting in front of their television sets watching themselves. The Rover's Return and Queen Vic would soon have to close down and perhaps reflect Princess Diana's desire to see less boozing on the box.*

It must be said that there are a few non-listeners among the *Guardian* readership and, to them, the incestuous correspondence about *The Archers* must get a bit galling. Every now and then some brave soul makes a stand against it, like this writer from Essex:

*I am intrigued by the esoteric correspondence dealing with the activities of **The Archers**. Is this the product of an exclusive inner circle happily engaged in taking in each other's washing? Or am I alone in never having listened to **The Archers**?*

Well, the statistics are on this writer's side. He is clearly not alone in never having listened to the programme but we do have enough evidence to convince us that he's part of the usually silent minority!

Another writer, this time from Hebden Bridge, gets equally cross and makes his point forcibly:

I am 70 years old and have never written to a national newspaper before but would like to make two wishes.

1 Editors used to have a weapon: 'This correspondence is now closed.' Could you use it with reference to Prue and Kenton and company?

2 Could you give M. Foot and A. Wedgwood-Benn each other's addresses and ask them to write direct to one another?

If you can grant me these two wishes and publish my letter, I promise not to write to you again (fingers crossed behind my back).

One can't help feeling some sympathy for the non-enthusiast . . . of *The Archers*, of course . . . I wouldn't dream of commenting on the exchanges between Michael Foot and Tony Benn!

Instead, let me pass on quickly to a gentleman from Piddlehinton in Dorset. He has a bee in his bonnet about the way Ambridge seems to have got closer to Birmingham in recent years:

*First we had Sid Perks banging on about coming from Birmingham, then we had Jack Woolley banging on and on about coming from Birmingham; next it was Mark and Shula banging on and on and on about working in Birmingham . . . unbelievably there is now some woman (Dawn?) banging on and on and on and on about Birmingham. I'm sick to death of your preoccupation with Birmingham. **The Archers** has become a semi-rural **Crossroads**.*

Steady on! We can take most insults thrown our way but comparison with *Crossroads* is going a bit far. I'm very tempted to play the role of censor on this letter but then, I suspect the writer is unaware of our sensitivity in relation to that particular soap opera, so I shall refrain from using the blue pencil and allow him to continue:

Ambridge is supposed to be somewhere near Evesham but do we ever hear Evesham, Worcester, Bristol, Gloucester, Stratford etc etc etc mentioned? No: your world is centred on Birmingham. (Perhaps you're funded by Birmingham Tourist Board?) Do we hear of the threat to rural post offices . . . shops . . . pubs . . . transport etc etc etc? Hardly at all. [Etc etc etc.]

That's a nice line about the Birmingham Tourist Board but the writer does have a point. He knows where his Ambridge is and by mentioning the big city too often, we are in danger of cutting off his line of imaginary retreat to the part of the countryside he prefers.

From a Mr Whitby of Bath, came another letter of criticism that hit a particularly tender spot: *What a con! After too many weeks of the Kenton Archer cliff-hanger, I now discover he has an overactive thyroid. Very thrilling.*

Archers *fans I know are fed up and angry at such a pathetic cop-out. We 25 to 40-year-olds have amused ourselves with speculation on the mystery illness. Could it be AIDS, a dark legacy of Merchant Navy life? What about cocaine, the champagne drug of the city yuppies? Or even ME, that unexplained new syndrome affecting hustling young go-getters? Nope, just a thyroid problem. Yawnsville.*

How many other listeners feel cheated by this latest whitewash? If I wasn't so hooked on Ambridge, I'd stop listening. **The Archers** *tackles all life's dramas, hence its endurance. Why shy away from an interesting conclusion that would have kept the scriptwriters busy for months to come?*
This spectre of AIDS in Ambridge created the kind of situation the seasoned BBC executive hates most, being in direct conflict with the programme-maker's editorial prerogative. In this instance, a combination of circumstances led to a difficult situation.

The storyline about Kenton's illness started just after Liz Rigbey had gone off on her sabbatical leave, when an acting editor was in charge and I was on holiday in Australia. When I got back, Kenton was already showing symptoms of a mysterious illness and, in honesty, I was impressed with a storyline that created a strong interest in a character notoriously difficult to involve in Ambridge life. One letter-writer from Fordingbridge was also enjoying it:
It is obvious that Kenton Archer is suffering from a bout of salmonella caused by eating Neil's eggs; listeria from Pat and Tony's live yoghurt and legionnaire's disease from the Grey Gables air conditioning system.

It wasn't until some weeks later that the penny dropped and I realised the way things were heading. Having presided over dozens of controversies during my 20 years of executive responsibility for the programme, I don't think anyone could accuse me of reluctance to go along with tackling tough issues (evidence Mr Whitby's own comments) but I wasn't ready for AIDS.

My view, for what it's worth, is that any discussion of such a savage and devastating disease needs to be handled with a sensitivity not possible in the cauldron of pub and village gossip. What would Eddie Grundy and Martha Woodford and Dave Barry and Tony Archer and Lynda Snell and Mrs Walker and all the others have made of Kenton Archer having AIDS? Would they have been rational and sympathetic? Would they have sought out Dr Thorogood for a reasoned medical opinion? Would they have given Kenton the benefit of the doubt about how he caught it?

Not on your life, they wouldn't. If they were being true to their characters, they would have created outrage and panic that would have dominated the village for a very, very long time.

Mr Whitby is right in feeling aggrieved about the way the storyline eventually developed and I have to take the responsibility for his feeling cheated. However, I don't believe there are too many other *Archers* listeners who would have found the AIDS story particularly entertaining and, rightly or wrongly, I decided it ought not to be allowed to develop.

How to stop it was quite another matter. Difficult as it is, I have long resisted the temptation to ask an editor to change a storyline and instead have relied on a mutual understanding about the nature of the programme and its listeners. At this point, there wasn't that kind of rapport (because of the temporary nature of the editor's appointment) and the plot was too far down the line for a casual conversation to be effective.

It was the press that came to my rescue. I got a call from a journalist who wanted to know one way or the other about Kenton's condition. I took our normal stance and said we didn't divulge storylines in advance, because we didn't want to upset regular listeners, and refused to give an answer. However,

They stop the mighty roar . . . Tony and Elizabeth Archer and Lucy Perks brought the bustling passengers to a halt for a few moments when they set up a smile stall at Euston station. It worked wonders. People smiled back.

when the reporter asked me off the record if he would look silly if he wrote that it was AIDS, I let him believe he would.

As a result, his story quoted 'an *Archers*' insider' and reported that Kenton did not have AIDS. Without me having to say a word to editor or writer, the message obviously got through and soon thereafter the danger passed and Kenton was found to be suffering from nothing more than thyroid trouble.

I like to think my stand was justified by the comment in a letter from a British exile in Denmark: 'I really think that if you had given Kenton AIDS, I would have thrown the radio out of the window.' However, in exchange for that one small crumb of comfort, I had to face a few more home truths as the disgruntled listener, a Mr Merrington, saw it:

I have listened to **The Archers** *for the last 25 years, give or take an Archer, and up to now have suffered in silence at the gradual conversion of Ambridge into a long-stay home for incurable social caricatures. Today's episode, however, was the straw that broke the camel's back.*

Why a loony-left vicar? Haven't we had enough

to put up with already? Lynda Snell, the unspeakable Jennifer and Elizabeth Archer, Tony and Pat and their sodding yoghurt, **tableau vivant** *from the lives of the saintly Grundys.*

If I wanted a rural edition of **Neighbours** *I could plaster the TV with cow dung and achieve much the same effect. If this is what life in the countryside is like, it's no wonder that most people live in the town.*

The whole point of **The Archers** *is not that it is socially relevant or even vaguely realistic but that it is there and, unlike everything about us in the world today, stays there in a warm, comfortable, welcoming form, hermetically removed from the so-called civilisation in which most of us are forced to live and work.*

It is an antidote to reality. The effect of trying to make it up-to-date, or whatever you think you are doing, is roughly the same as putting ground glass in a headache powder. I really think that if you had given *Kenton AIDS, I would have thrown the radio out of the window.*

What kind of insane, warped logic could ever have come up with the idea that people can be entertained by listening to other people moaning on about imaginary 'real life' problems. I've got quite enough real 'real life' problems of my own, thank you.

The truth of the matter is that agriculture is now a high-pressure, industrial pursuit inextricably enmeshed in a system of subsidies which penalise rational, ecological methods of production. It is also one of the largest generators of water pollution in northern Europe.

The small farmers are going to the wall and the large ones are all running animal concentration camps. If you think you can make all that into entertainment, then you are, in my opinion, quite mad. At any rate, if you are going to try then you have to get rid of all those unbearable, cardboard cut-out, clichéd figures who inhabit Ambridge at the moment.

People like Walter Gabriel and Dan Archer were at their most acceptable in two dimensions because they represented mythical elements of society – nobody ever assumed that they existed other than in their own right. They summed up ideas and values in concentrated form, like the masked characters in classical Chinese and Japanese theatre.

However, people like Lynda Snell (and now this absurd vicar) are merely badly drawn caricatures motivated by an implied common social prejudice. We are supposed to think that they are 'just like . . .' and then supply the name of our own personal offending bugbear. It doesn't work.

A myth does not need nuances because the characters it contains are archetypes; a caricature or a parody (as many of the most-used characters have become) does. Look at the differences between Uncle Tom and Bert. People who, in real life, exemplify such undiluted manic traits as many of the current Ambridge folk, are usually found in psychiatric hospitals.

If you want realism, then make it real!

With a programme as widely listened to as *The Archers*, you simply can't win. If we did as Mr Merrington suggested, we would immediately alienate that other half of the audience represented by Mrs Taylor of Lancashire:

In my opinion, you are allowing too much aggravation to creep into **The Archers** *lately.* **I** *do not listen to or watch any soaps except* **The Archers***, to which I have been listening since I retired in 1981. For me, it is pure* **escapism** *and I like it to be as life* **should** *be, and not as life* **is***.*

I did not like today's episode one bit. I don't want any break-up of the two young marriages. What I would like your scriptwriters to do is to have Ruth get pregnant and come back home and to bring Shula and Mark together so that they can bring forth young in a year or two.

It I were you, I should not engage any scriptwriters who have themselves been in the abyss of divorce, since I think they would have a natural tendency to let their own misfortunes stray into the storyline.

Mercifully for the writers, the BBC management takes a more liberal attitude and we don't enquire about people's marital status when we invite them to join the team.

From Alcester in Worcestershire, another lady writes with more advice for the writers:

I have listened to **The Archers** *since the very first episode and would like to continue to do so. However, would the scriptwriters take Jennifer in hand. The time is long overdue when she should have her comeuppance and be reminded of the fact that she is a publican's daughter and not one of the Lawson-Hopes. It would be even better if the scales were lifted from her eyes and she could see her husband for the womaniser he is.*

She goes on to comment about the personality defects of Lynda Snell and Elizabeth Archer and ends with a heartfelt plea:

I know it's just a story but we do listen for pleasure and not to have the worries of the world rammed down our throats. Oh for the old days of the Tregorrans.

Harsh as some of the criticisms are, there is no one associated with the programme who would want to see any lessening of the commitment so many listeners obviously feel. It is, above all, their programme and it's only right that they should have the opportunity to make their voices heard.

CHAPTER EIGHT

WHAT THE PAPERS SAY

*You cannot hope
to bribe or twist,
thank God! the
British journalist.
But, seeing what
the man will do
unbribed, there's
no occasion to.*

Humbert Wolfe

IT'S NOT SOMETHING TO be admitted lightly and certainly not spoken about too loudly . . . but *The Archers* is very much indebted to Britain's journalists and that most maligned of our national institutions, the press. Since the very beginning, in 1951, there has been a strong newspaper interest in the programme, and Tony Shryane, the first producer, has the most astonishing collection of cuttings from the 28 years he was in charge.

Today, the production office at Pebble Mill is constantly inundated with clippings from newspapers all over Britain and regularly has to transfer great bundles of them to libraries and archives units. This, I should add, is a very small price to pay for the way the programme has benefited, particularly in recent years, from the continuing interest and almost universal affection of the press. On the occasions when criticisms have been made, we've learned to shrug our shoulders and accept the principles of a free pass . . . even if, sometimes, it's through clenched teeth!

It's a delicate relationship and we know only too well that the balance can tip against us at any moment. There's always the danger of popularity turning sour and we could quickly become the new whipping-boy for a sensation-hungry press. Alternatively, we must sometimes get very close to being boring in newspaper terms, which could lead to our being completely ignored. Those who subscribe to the theory (and I'm not one of them) that there's no such thing as bad publicity would probably say

that the latter risk is more serious than the former.

While we have never been exactly shy about telling journalists what is going on in and around *The Archers*, we don't actually court them. We are usually – but not always – happy to give our time for long interviews or photo sessions and we never complain when they turn into very small items in the paper or when the proposed articles or pictures never appear at all.

The one irritant in the relationship is the presence of a mole in our team. In an effort to keep faith with the listeners, the one area we never discuss is the development of future storylines. We don't want to give anything away that might interfere with the audience's enjoyment of the programme. There is someone within our ranks who doesn't share that philosophy and I have been angered over the years by the regular leaking of script information to the press. One cannot blame journalists for taking and using the stories they're fed by the insider but the culprit must have a warped sense of responsibility – happy to take our money but not to stick to the rules.

It was the miserable mole who made me forget one of the basic principles when talking to journalists – always be quite clear when you're talking off the record. The short-lived magazine, *Riva*, got wind of our intention to bring in a celebrity guest and the reporter, Geoff Baker (an old friend of mine), managed to circumvent our press enquiries routine and spoke to me direct. I'll let him tell the

rest of the story, as he did to *Riva* readers:
Dum dee dum dee dum deesaster! Stand by your wireless. Ambridge is in turmoil. A VIP is coming to town and Elizabeth hasn't got a thing to wear! The BBC is bubbling with its own cleverness, having persuaded an SVBI (Somebody Very Big Indeed) to join the existing cast of **The Archers**.

I probably was feeling too clever because I thought I had played a straight bat to all his attempts to wheedle the name out of me.
Is it Joan Collins? Mick Jagger? Or will Prince Charles follow Auntie Margaret's lead and drive down from his Cotswolds pile for a jar of Prue Forrest's WI-beating jam? Give us a clue, Jock. 'Nope. And I'll chew the balls off anyone who tells you,' says the charming Scot.
He added to the indignity of my off-the-cuff retort by revealing that the guest was to be Dame Edna Everage . . . and we still haven't caught the mole!

Needless to say, the press don't always stick to the rules of fair play and accuracy. I was alarmed one Sunday last year when I saw a billboard outside my local newsagent declaring that the *People* was carrying a story about how 'The Archers create chaos in the air.' When I rushed in to buy the paper, I finally found a paragraph:
Pilots are having trouble landing their planes . . . because of the top radio soap **The Archers**.

Their instruments are sent spinning by tales of the Ambridge folk as they approach Staverton Airport, near Gloucester.

How, you might ask? What was Eddie Grundy up to now? For once, Eddie and his cohorts were blameless . . . and so was the programme, as the second paragraph revealed:
The BBC's Radio 4 transmitter in nearby Droitwich is interfering with guidance systems at the airport and planes are being sent up to 15 degrees off course.
Such is the price of notoriety that of all the radio programmes broadcast on the Droitwich transmitter it was *The Archers* that was named.

It's amazing how sensitive some people are about what they hear on the programme and even more surprising how quickly the press get on to the people who are upset. When we introduced one of our hitherto silent characters and let him speak, we immediately landed in hot water . . . or should that be hot fat?

It all started innocently enough. The French chef at Grey Gables, Jean-Paul, was reminiscing about his earlier experiences in British kitchens and referred to his time in Leeds. Then, as the *Yorkshire Post* put it:
Surprise turned to annoyance in some quarters when the culinary prima donna claimed people in Leeds cooked their chips in pig fat.

Last night Mr David Mitchell, the manager of one of Leeds' best-known fish and chip restaurants, Bryan's, retorted: 'This is certainly not true. We and 99 per cent of fish and chip restaurants in Yorkshire use beef dripping. This is what the Yorkshire taste requires.'

In the best traditions of the press, the *Yorkshire Post* invited us to give our side of the story and that really put us on the spot. We apologised for Jean-Paul's lapse and explained:
This is the very first time he has been allowed outside the kitchen and we will have to think very hard before we allow him out again. He wouldn't know the difference between a faggot and a black pudding.
When I gave the comment to our press office, I thought it was quite witty but seeing it printed in the sober columns of the paper and attributed to a BBC spokesman I wished I hadn't put my tongue in my cheek!

Having set ourselves up as experts on rural life, it's quite natural that we are then sitting ducks for any expert who wants to point out one of our gaffes. *Country File* magazine was more than happy to do that:
What is going on at Ambridge? In recent weeks, Borchester's blackbirds and song thrushes have been singing as if spring was already here, and not five months away, while only a month ago a lapwing was heard giving its typical spring territorial display over the pastures of Old Court Farm. Strangely the ever-observant Tom Forrest doesn't seem to have noticed. Perhaps **The Archers** *have become too concerned with organic yoghurt to notice unseasonal birds.*

Up to our necks in it, we were! We were also threatened by a deluge of letters from egg producers by that friendly little specialist publication, the Grocer:

*As part of my world-renowned service of being helpful to all and sundry, I have important news for the producer of that beloved, everyday radio story of countryfolk, **The Archers**. For the BBC executive is set to receive a tidal wave of mail in the coming weeks – with most of the extra in the form of advice from Britain's beleaguered egg producers.*

The shell-shocked eggmen, battered and bruised from the salmonella scare which has blighted their lives for three months, rang their own alarms this week on hearing rumours that the issue was to be a topic on the famous programme.

And to ensure that the industry line was heard by those whose job it is to create the lives of Britain's most famous farming family, that worthy body the UK Egg Producers Association has circulated the BBC producer's official address to its members.

Since the Association numbers over 700 farmers, the Post Office sorting centre at Pebble Mill district look like being busier than usual during the next few weeks!

Forewarned, we were forearmed and were able to cope with the six letters that eventually arrived. I suspect, at that time, the poor eggmen had much more important things on their minds than writing to us.

One of the shrewdest observers of the Ambridge scene is Gillian Reynolds of the *Daily Telegraph*. She writes about the programme with an affection that never becomes sentimental. Like us, she is in constant search of the key to the mystery of Ambridge's appeal. Unlike us, she is unbiased and can look at the programme objectively. While we fondly imagine that the success is largely due to our Herculean efforts, Gillian has a much simpler idea to offer her readers:

It was television, some believe, which brought Ambridge out of its mysterious shadows and into the media glare. By becoming progressively frantic and tedious, lower-browed and loud over the past five years, early evening TV has driven people to search radio for reassuring draughts of normality. People who would not dream of tuning into Radios 1 and 2 for fear of losing their street credibility suddenly

discovered the lost world of Ambridge on Radio 4.

This neatly coincided with a fashion for dressing up to look like your grandparents: sturdy country squire for young men, GI bride reborn for girls. A village where time had stood still – apart from a bit of heavy breathing on Lakey Hill (from Shula and Mark) – was just the thing. Ambridge was colonised at once by a new audience.

Does that, I wonder, make the new listener a middle-class young fogey who tunes into the early-evening episode while driving the company's souped-up Cavalier to pick up his Sloane-Ranger girlfriend? If so, I'm sure Gillian would join me in bidding them welcome, nevertheless.

Gillian also reveals her strong protective instincts towards the programme when she warns off would-be meddlers:

The serial has even fallen into the clammy grip of Academe. There are lecturers at obscure universities who now offer their services as unofficial archivists and agricultural specialists. Perhaps this very weekend final touches are being put on theses proving Mrs Perkins is a symbol of collective urban working-class consciousness or that 'The Village Pump', Tom Forrest's perpetually unfinished party piece, has its roots in Turnip Townshend [sic] and the Agricultural Revolution.

*Ten years ago, Jonathan Raban said in **The Listener** that the serial is 'Radio's own demotic **Iliad**,' with much of the content of a magazine 'while never losing the essential veneer, at least, of dramatic fiction'. Pure radio, he called it.*

Val Gielgud, the founding father of BBC radio drama, assessed it rather differently back in 1951. 'Acceptable hokum,' he said.

Now, who should I agree with? The erudite Jonathan Raban or the vastly experienced Val Gielgud? Who does Gillian Reynolds agree with? I suspect we would both go along with both of them!

The search for the answer to the programme's success is a bit like that for the Holy Grail but every now and again someone is convinced they've found it. Like Merseyside's *Daily Post*, for example:

*Many sociologists and others have suggested explanations for the enduring popularity of **The Archers**.*

No doubt a nostalgic longing for an idyllic

rustic past has something to do with it (though the writers try their best to inject all sorts of unlikely contemporary ills into the script), but **The Archers** *popularity is surely as simple as its setting.*

It is a pleasant interlude in a busy day, or perhaps a lonely day, for an audience that feels it knows the residents of Ambridge at least as well as it knows the people across the road. And, because of the nature of radio, **The Archers** *characters exist most vividly in the imagination of each and every listener.*

I have long since given up trying to find explanations but that one rather appeals to me.

The search for success in a totally different area – business – led the *Kettering Evening Telegraph* back to Ambridge. At the start of a new year, writer Lester Cowling set himself the task of discovering the key to business success. None of your realism here. Mr Cowling had obviously had enough of the fast-talking millionaires of Northamptonshire. He talked instead to none other than Borsetshire's Mr Jack Woolley:

Mr Woolley is almost part of the British subconscious – the self-made man who sold up his Birmingham business to settle down in Ambridge and run his Grey Gables country club-cum-hotel.

The paper then went on to give the 'Grey Gables Key to Success' ... be nice to the customers, provide a quality service, don't listen to your underlings (especially if he's a half-mad French chef), look after the pennies and so on and so on.

In what appears to be a regular feature about the landed gentry, the *Stately Homes and Gardens* magazine headlined their piece 'The Fortunes of Nigel', and there, large as life, was the elegant Nigel Pargetter looking to-the-manor-born in the grounds of a splendid pile. The caption said it was Loxley Hall:

There are 12 acres of land adjoining the Hall, comprising walled garden, formal garden and an arboretum which was planted by Nigel's great-grandfather. The estate, although shrunk by half when death duties forced sale for development, still runs to nearly 2500 acres. There are seven farms, more than 300 acres of woodland, dwellings including an attractive dower house, 35 assorted cottages and 11 other houses for staff.

Country Living magazine (edited by Francine Lawrence, a very keen listener to *The Archers*) blurred the lines between fact and fantasy even further by commissioning the pseudonymous Bruno Milna (in reality Norman Painting, who also plays Phil Archer) to interview Shula Archer (Phil's daughter, who is now actually Mrs Shula Hebden) about her country childhood. I was surprised to find that Shula hadn't liked life in and around Ambridge when she was a youngster. Funny, that – she'd never mentioned it before:

There was a time when I hated the countryside and everything to do with it. Not just when I was standing in the wet, waiting for the school bus; or when I was scraping the mud off my walking shoes (I seemed to spend half my life doing that), but always. The countryside to me wasn't wide open spaces, birdsong and fresh air: it was a barrier between me and where I thought I really wanted to be.

However, she did enjoy the reminiscences of older Ambridge folk like her grandparents, Dan and Doris Archer, and old Walter Gabriel, who were all children of the pre-radio days:

Compared with the life I was leading in the countryside, with its commuting and its permissiveness, its noise and its anxieties about the environment and the Third World, their country childhood had a gentleness and a contentment and an innocence that seemed worlds away.

I wonder if mine will seem like that to my children?

It's just as well Shula had a column all to herself in *Country Living* because she didn't get a mention in that contemporary culinary guide, *Good Food Fast*. On their 'Fast Country Menus' page, the magazine homed in on our favourite village:

All students of Ambridge will know that food and drink are used as a shorthand to denote a character's social standing – from upper-class twit Nigel Pargetter swigging champagne to the regulars at The Bull downing pints of Shires.

Not all of us had stopped to consider such a vital matter but, on reflection, we should be grateful for being reminded that we have a very handy script device up our sleeves:

Kathy Perks underestimated local resistance to

change when she tried to revamp *The Bull's* bar menu; Persian chicken, fisherman's pie and an effete assortment of quiches didn't cut much ice and Clarrie scorned the kiwi fruit ('looks like a mouldy peach'). Tom Forrest was banished to the spare bedroom by Prue after indulging in the garlic mushrooms and was relieved to return to a ploughman's lunch – with or without Lymeswold cheese – introduced by Clarrie in a rare innovative mood.

At Grey Gables, well-heeled tourists and the **nouveaux riches** tuck into Jean-Paul's legendary pastry, while on Grange Farm those ultimate low-lifers, the Grundys, get frozen TV dinners or, if Clarrie is feeling confident, home-made dumplings. Ideology rears its head at Bridge Farm, where Pat Archer compels her luckless brood to eat her attempts at low-fat, organic yoghurt, though she has given up trying to make them nibble organic carrots instead of sweets.

Jennifer Aldridge agonises over her dinner-party menus at Home Farm – venison is a particular favourite – but strive as she may for social triumph, she fails to see how gauche it is to employ a cleaning lady like the snobbish Mrs Walker, sipping her coffee essence and nibbling her gypsy creams. Poor Jennifer Aldridge does come in for a lot of stick for being so naive underneath that hard exterior. At least she doesn't have to put up with Mrs Walker any more. She's moved on to terrorise someone else.

If all these magazines can't see the joins in the scripts, surely a good solid newspaper like the *Shropshire Star* won't be confused. Or will it? *Shirley Tart was at the Albert Hall for the WI AGM and met Betty Tucker from the long-running radio show* **The Archers**, *or did she?*

Quite bright of the sub-editor, I thought, leaving the clever stuff, like providing the answers, to the writer who gets the big by-line: *Did Betty have a new frock for the occasion, I asked Pam. She said: 'Well actually she got this little suit from Oxfam for £3.50. I didn't have the sort of clothes that Betty might wear so I bought this from the Oxfam shop – in Richmond, not Borchester. It's an Eastex and Betty could never have afforded to buy that new. Though she's a bit upset about her*

shoes. She broke the heel on her courts so she's had to wear these flatties.' She waved a foot at me. 'She's a bit embarrassed about that.'

Was she saying that she (Pamela) bought a suit from Oxfam so that Betty could go to the WI annual meeting in some sort of style? She assured me, eyeball-to-eyeball, that she was and she had.

'Mind you, Pat (in the series) lent me the hat!' She produced a large-brimmed straw affair and added: 'Pat has hats because she goes to a lot of weddings but Betty's hoping she won't have to wear it. She'll feel very self-conscious if she does.'

Who was she speaking as now, Pam or Betty? 'Both,' she said, her face still as straight as her bobbed hair.

At that point I more or less gave up trying to work out the relationship between Pamela and her alter-ego.

I know the feeling of confusion only too well. Everyone associated with *The Archers* suffers from it from time to time. I seem to spend a great deal of time apologising for calling the actors by their characters' names, and introducing them to visitors on formal occasions can be a bit of a nightmare.

However, Shirley Tart was much less confused than one national newspaper figure, who shall remain nameless. Some years ago, we produced a Doris Archer fudge and because it was being packaged in the home-made style, I asked Gwen Berryman if she would write 'Doris Archer' in her handwriting to be used on the wrapper. Gwen did so cheerfully and then asked me how much commission she would get out of letting the company use her name. I had to point out that it wasn't actually *her* name. When I used the story some time later, to illustrate this very problem of confusion, the journalist concerned looked at me in total bewilderment. He never did get the point!

Someone else who will probably never get the point is the bemused Australian who, the Peterborough column in the *Daily Telegraph* told us, firmly believes the programme is a British Secret Service broadcast: *A colleague recalls how an Australian some years ago was initially scathing about Britain's daily love affair with the rustics of Ambridge. Then at a party, a wag who had obviously* been in The Bull, whispered the little known fact that **The Archers** was actually an MI5/MI6 coded transmission. The phrase: 'I counted 14 sheep on Lakey Hill' meant, for example, that agents one to 14 should rendezvous.

After that the visitor became a devout student of the programme. Back in Perth, he still fondly believes he knows something the Poms do not.

Another of our Fleet Street fans is Geoffrey Smith, news editor of the Press Association. Geoff has listened to the programme since it ousted his old favourite, Dick Barton, from the airwaves. He is a walking encyclopaedia about The Archers and his features appear in the major provincial newspapers all over Britain.

One of his articles included a specially commissioned plan showing how the proposed bypass feeder road would have affected Ambridge and this very handy guide to what the cast think of the characters they play:

Patricia Greene on **Jill Archer**: 'She is a bit too good. I keep trying to invest her with a little more reality and I recently had a scene where I was allowed to blow my top. That's very rare.'

Norman Painting on **Phil Archer**: 'He was a bighead, a ram but he has always had a heart as big as a bucket because he is an Archer and he loves the whole family.'

Patricia Gallimore on **Pat Archer**: 'I admire her for standing up for women's rights and working hard. She went through a phase of being ultra-feminist but that has been toned down now and she is more realistic.'

Alison Dowling on **Elizabeth Archer**: 'Witty, entertaining and inside she has a good heart. She is the youngest and I always think the youngest have a hard time proving themselves because they are battling for attention all the time.'

Tracy-Jane White on **Lucy Perks**: 'She has some good ideas but she blows hot and cold on the flavour of the month.'

Jack May on **Nelson Gabriel**: 'He is a great fun character, providing a sort of counterpoint in the programme. All this about being a bad hat is not really true. I have always thought he is a fairly decent chap.'

Nigel Carrington on **Nigel Pargetter**: 'He is

nice and caring and very community-minded. He has too much going for him to become an eccentric fossil. He is older now but he does not lose his sense of fun.'

Colin Skipp on **Tony Archer**: 'He used to be a womaniser before he became settled. I always feel jealous of Tony because he is so secure and happy.'

Carole Boyd on **Lynda Snell**: 'She has much more scope now than at the beginning. There is more room for her relationship with her husband to be explored. She is very misunderstood. Deep down she is vulnerable.'

Edward Kelsey on **Joe Grundy**: 'I think he is vastly misunderstood. He has a heart of gold but the trouble is he does not want anyone to know that.'

Mollie Harris on **Martha Woodford**: 'She is a kind person; she's not just a malicious gossip. She just passes it on.'

Sam Barriscale on **John Archer**: 'He is a bit of a sadist in the way he likes all the illnesses the animals get.'

Sadly for Geoffrey Smith, his direct contact with all the actors has interfered too much with his imagination for him to go on enjoying the programme at the same level as before.

That's the danger Antonia Swinson faced when she persuaded us to let her join the cast (she's also an actress) to write an inside piece for the Sunday Express Magazine. She was lucky:

Despite my look behind the scenes, the show's magic hasn't died. Though my head tells me they're just actors working in the studio, earning money for their mortgages in Islington or Lancaster, something suspends my disbelief.

For Ambridge **does** exist. With some strange alchemy, the actors' voices float across the airwaves and become **The Archers**. They are real people, as real as the man down the road, or the person we sit next to on the bus. More so, for they are a part of our innermost life. We grow old as they do, we too are written out of the story. Those anonymous voices bear a heavy responsibility.

It was, once again, Gillian Reynolds of the Daily Telegraph who underlined that responsibility:

It is a well-established fact that anything happening in the real world only becomes really real when it happens in Ambridge.

What would you do, for instance, if the minister sent to perform your marriage were a woman? David and Ruth Archer tackled this one last November. How to cope with teenagers, the problems of aged parents, the residential development of the countryside, the agonies of local politics – the range of social concerns on **The Archers** *has never been wider. From rat infestation at Grey Gables to prohibitive meddling by English Heritage in the restoration of Loxley Hall – the listener feels that if Jack and Nigel can get on with it the rest of us can too.*

There are three levels on which all of this must work. First, gossip (why does Dr Thorogood want to develop his outbuilding?). Second, official propaganda (here are the rules on notification of animal diseases). Third, the deeply social (was the old vicar right to marry the divorced George to Christine in church?).

Controversial questions (what's wrong with building new houses in the village?) tend to be presented initially from a bold point of view, with the balancing arguments introduced gradually over the weeks that follow. Given the due impartiality which the BBC is often instructed these days to observe (remember the scandal when Mark stood as SDP candidate?) and that scripts come from diverse hands, occasioning the odd fluctuation in character, it's a wonder they manage to tackle so much.

The issue that is set to develop most intensely over the next few months is that of childlessness. Should Shula and Mark settle for a marriage with no natural offspring (plenty of advice to take here from Auntie Christine, Uncle Tom, Martha Woodfood, Jack Woolley, the woman who breeds dogs and that nosey Mrs Snell) or should they keep trying? It is a question that dramatists and documentary makers have addressed in the past, but in the homelier context of **The Archers** *perhaps the complex issues can get across more clearly.*

The *Guardian*, however, was more concerned about the very simple issue of Prue Forrest. Was she alive and well and living in Ambridge or was she not? The matter became too important to leave to the letter-writers. A strong editorial was what was needed . . . and that's what we got:

Aficionados of **The Archers**, *a notoriously edgy crew, have been thronging our letters page this week to inquire into the prolonged and unexplained silence of Prue Forrest, wife of the unspeakable Tom. Some believe she has not said a word these 30 years. Others have detected expletives like 'shush' (a rebuke to her husband for speaking in church) or 'aargh' (an instinctive reaction when confronted on her eightieth birthday with a cake she had not expected). Only one of our correspondents claims to have heard a whole sentence. Asked some time ago if she felt proud to have won a jam-making competition, he alleges, Prue replied: 'Yes, I am proud, very proud.'*

We could have been dismissive of this claim for it was wholly erroneous but then that would have spoiled a good editorial. So we were more than happy when the writer went on to chronicle some of the other possible explanations for Mrs Forrest's speechlessness:

Three readers in London WC2 allege that Prue is so drunk that she cannot get to the microphone. This may be the sort of condition which is commonplace in WC2 but it would not have gone unremarked in Ambridge. Some gnarled buffoon would surely have cause to remark that her triumph in home-making was all the greater for being achieved while smashed. That sort of thing may not be much of a hazard while growing prize marrows but it does tend to blur the judgment while one is baking cakes.

Alternatively the explanation may lie in the BBC casting department and that the actress who originally created Prue has been too busy since with more demanding assignments to spare time for Ambridge. (Her identity is unknown: a trawl of the curriculum vitae of say, Glenda Jackson or Judi Dench might conceivably be rewarding.) Even so, while we have that one crystal line available in the archives, producers of wit and experience ought still to be able to make far more of Prue. You can do quite a lot with a single consistent response. 'I am proud, very proud' would serve as a suitable answer to many a poignant question of current controversy. 'As one who once carried a torch for the late Clement Davies,' Jill Archer might ask her, for instance, 'how do you feel about Captain Paddy's triumph?' and the ancient crone would reply 'I am proud, very proud.' Indeed some clever splicing, wedding the odd expletive to her one recorded utterance, might widen her range still further. How is her physical state as she enters her ninth decade, the vicar might ask solicitously. 'I am bowed, very bowed,' she would tell him. And how, above all, does she feel when accused in a national daily of perpetual and hopeless drunkenness? 'Cowed, very cowed,' she'd reply.

The *Guardian* leader-writer showed considerable prescience in linking Dame Judi Dench with Prue more than eight months before she accepted the role for the ten thousandth episode!

The Listener, once a BBC publication but now independently owned, still has proprietorial tendencies, and radio critic, Nigel Andrew, is strongly resistant to even a hint of change. Somebody, somewhere got the wrong end of the stick and Nigel used it to beat us at a time whe we were celebrating the ten thousandth episode and, admittedly, making quite a noise:

*There has been a frankly terrifying report that some sort of link is to be forged between **The Archers** and **EastEnders** via Mrs P. This (if true) is sheer insanity: in Ambridge, television doesn't even exist. I hope this has nothing to do with the newly appointed editor, Ruth Patterson.*

Well, it didn't have anything to do with Ruth. It was something that came up before she arrived on the scene and the thought was not to link the two programmes directly in the way that Nigel Andrew feared. The idea was that one of the residents of Albert Square would turn out to be the daughter of an old friend of Mrs P. and would come to visit her in Ambridge. *EastEnders* would never have been mentioned and it would have been left as a joke for our most ardent fans. Unaware of all this, Nigel Andrews offered this advice to Ruth:

*She must know that **The Archers** is at its best when it is left to trundle along under its own momentum, without sudden lurches into high drama and low comedy, without contrived situations and publicity-inspired gimmicks. The great strength of **The Archers** is in its characters, so firmly established now as to seem rather more real than many a 'real-life' person. They must be handled with respect and, essentially, left to get on with being themselves. **The Archers** got where it is, not by*

publicity stunts but by being true to itself, week in, week out (despite some alarming wobbles over the years). It has nothing to prove, and no need to lower itself, least of all in the quest for a younger audience – of which it already has a bigger share than almost any other Radio 4 regular. I sincerely hope that once the hype has died down, things will get back on course and we shall again hear the 'Tum-ti tum-ti tum-ti-tum . . .' without instinctively cringing.

Even before I could spring to the defence of the new editor, Richard Last in the *Daily Telegraph* had done it for me. Perhaps he had followed the adage that you shouldn't believe everything you read in the papers and he tackled Ruth direct about her plans for the future of the programme:

*Before the massed legions of **Archers** fans – rather more than seven million at the last count – rumble into action, let me hastily make clear that Miss Patterson comes not to bring the sword of revolution, but the ploughshare of progress. As an **Archers** fan for ten out of her 28 years, she knows perfectly well that you do not lay violent hands upon a priceless piece of the nation's heritage.*

'I admit I came into the job with the bit between my teeth. But I knew in my heart of hearts that radical change was not what anyone wanted. I knew it would take at least a year before the writing could go the way I wanted it to go.'

Patterson arrived at a time of trauma but she was well equipped to cope. She has degrees in English and film, a remarkable amount of TV and radio experience packed into her three years with the BBC, and the gritty determination associated with the natives of Yorkshire.

*Patterson worries that the programme sometimes gets the relative prominence of its documentary strands out of balance with the drama. 'What draws people to **The Archers** is the strength of the characters,' she says decisively.*

She might well have added that it's also the strength of the production team and the writers and the actors . . . with a little bit of help from our friends in the press:

*Richard Fernley [an **Independent** reader] worked as a communications officer in the Royal Fleet Auxiliary with a captain who often remarked: 'Bugger the NATO exercise, let's get **The Archers**.'*

CHAPTER NINE

EPISODE 10 000

IT TOOK NEARLY 30 million words to get there . . . but it was worth it. The build-up to the historic ten thousandth episode – broadcast on Friday, 26 May 1989 – and all the celebrations that surrounded it, underlined the place *The Archers* holds in the affections of millions of people in Britain, even among those who insist that they never listen.

Certainly, there can't be many who didn't know it was happening. The series of events organised to mark the occasion attracted so much attention – heightened by the coincidental announcement of Ruth Patterson's appointment as the new editor – that the radio press officer at Pebble Mill, Alan Cooke, started talking about weighing the newspaper cuttings instead of simply measuring the column inches!

Alan also came to an arrangement with the Royal Mail whereby every letter posted in any pillar box or at any post office in the fortnight before the celebrations would be franked with a special postmark giving the date of the historic broadcast. That added up to a spectacular 600 million letters. We also produced our own commemorative cover which, with the addition of the special Food and Farming Year stamps, proved very popular both with listeners and philatelists.

We enticed Terry Wogan into visiting Ambridge, by way of recompense for all the rude things he'd said about the programme during his days on Radio 2. After all, it was his blarney that had started all the wonderful stories about the where-abouts of the silent Prue Forrest. As a bit of fun, we decided to cast Prue and give her and Terry a conversation in the ten thousandth episode. And we were delighted when Dame Judi Dench entered into the spirit of the occasion and accepted the role. For good measure, we recruited Esther Rantzen (a former studio manager) to do the sound effects.

The *Radio Times* responded by putting *The Archers* on the front cover for the first time since Shula's wedding and BBC Television's *40 Minutes* series joined in the celebrations by starting a long-term filming project. The interest proved to be worldwide and we had journalists and photographers coming to Birmingham from a variety of countries. One of my most difficult moments came when an American television crew arrived at Pebble Mill with a modest ambition . . . 'to unravel the mystery of how, in the age of television, a radio programme can capture the minds and hearts of the British nation'.

The reporter's opening question was direct and simple: 'Can you tell me your secret?' Finding an answer was, of course, far from simple . . . and it got worse. 'Can you explain the relationships of the villagers for our audience?' With visions of oilmen in Dallas, lawmen in Miami, taxi-drivers in New York, and the Beverly Hills mob, I realised I was on a hiding to nothing. They would never grasp that the quaintly named Mrs P. was . . . mother to Peggy Archer; grandmother to Tony Archer, Lilian Bellamy and Jennifer Aldridge; great-grandmother

Don't call us . . . Esther Rantzen returned to her broadcasting roots for the ten thousandth episode of The Archers *in May 1989. She created the sound effects while a certain Irish gentleman played himself, alongside Dame Judi Dench's memorable Prue Forrest. The experience of meeting a television superstar proved too much for the retiring Prue and when she spoke in the wrong place, she vowed never to speak in public again . . . not even for the twenty thousandth episode!*

to Helen, John and Tommy Archer, James Bellamy, Adam Travers-Macy, Deborah, Kate and Alice Aldridge; and related to almost half the village by marriage!

Sitting in the shade of a leafy tree in the grounds of Pebble Mill, the reporter was clearly transported to Ambridge and wanted to know about our great silent majority . . . the villagers who are never heard . . . Higgs, Jean Harvey, Mrs Bagshaw, Snatch Foster, the Horrobins, Godfrey Wendover *et al.* If I had been addressing a British audience, it would have been easy to talk about creating the illusion of scale, giving the village a

viable community. But would the cowboys of Arizona get their ropes around that?

I assumed the end result would be so bewildering to the American audience that it would never see the light of day but I got two letters from people who had seen it in America. Both were British, however, so we never did find out what the Americans made of the exploits of Eddie Grundy, Elizabeth Archer and Nelson Gabriel!

The celebrations for the cast and production team began at lunchtime on the eve of the ten thousandth episode – the Thursday – in the unlikely arena of London's Euston station. British Rail were naming a new locomotive *Royal Show*, and *The Archers* (with our long association with Europe's biggest agricultural event) were invited to help at the launching ceremony. Most of the cast turned out to watch Norman Painting and the chairman of the Royal Agricultural Society of England, Charles Smith-Ryland, unveil the traditional

Press drama . . . The BBC's head of radio drama, John Tydeman (godfather to The Archers) *explains why he's at Euston station to the Guardian's Val Arnold-Forster and the Daily Telegraph's Gillian Reynolds, two of the programme's strongest supporters.*

The Intercity slickers . . . Waxed jackets and wellies were left behind for this day out in London and it was very much a group of professional actors who helped launch the new Intercity diesel locomotive, Royal Show, at Euston station.

plaque on the Class 90 locomotive 90009. A small orchestra played 'Barwick Green', the champagne corks popped, the cameras clicked and the usually weary travellers stopped to look on and smile at the 'countryfolk' come to town.

There were also celebrations around the country. At Lanlivery, near Bodmin in Cornwall, the locals turned their village into Ambridge for the day; and in Griffithstown, Gwent, the Vicar of St Hilda's and St Oswald's held a thanksgiving service.

The Reverend Dr Raymond Bayley said that he was disappointed when speakers at an earlier

Welcome home . . . The rumbustious Godfrey Baseley made his first visit to Pebble Mill for many years and was soon telling the head of broadcasting, David Waine, what he thought about that day's programme. Fortunately he enjoyed it!

All styles . . . er, smiles . . . Jack Woolley, Jill Archer and David show that Ambridge knows where it's at! They've been reading Francine Lawrence's Country Living magazine and can even keep up with the avant garde Zandra Rhodes.

meeting of the Church of Wales governing body had criticised soap operas as poor-quality programming: 'On the contrary, they provide some of the best-written socially conscious drama available and they should really be described as continuing life dramas!' *The Archers*, said Dr Bayley, was the noblest of these dramas. In its 10 000 episodes it had shown the trials, triumphs and tragedies of a rural community and its church.

For those more directly involved with the programme, however, the main celebration was a banquet at the Pebble Mill studios. Unfortunately there was room for only 120 guests – the ticket touts could have made a fortune – and the lucky ones were there as representatives of wider groups.

In a toast to the guests, I explained why each group had been invited. The cast were there as the front-line troops, the actors and actresses who make flesh the characters that people Ambridge and give the performances so crucial to the listeners' enjoyment of the programme.

The writers, of course, put words into people's mouths, and create the platform from which the actors launch their splendid performances. I've always thought that the writers' contracts should carry government health warnings because of the strain of constantly staring at a blank sheet of paper ... or, even worse, gazing at a blank word-processor screen.

Important as the actors and the writers are, it's the editors and producers who skilfully shape their contributions to give us the actual programmes. Especially welcome guests were the programme's first production assistant, Valerie Shryane; the first producer, Tony Shryane; and the originator and creator, Godfrey Baseley, who fought all the necessary battles to launch *The Archers* on the world 10 000 episodes earlier. They were given a standing ovation.

Then there were the unsung heroes, the audio staff ... the brilliant technicians and operators who translate the producers' artistic whims into radio. They are the experts who can help the listeners' imagination soar with exactly the right sound effect in the right place at the right time.

While the audio unit creates much of the magic in the studio, there are a fair few miracles performed regularly in the production office. Between them, the secretaries and production assistants cope with the deluge of listeners who ring or write in looking for information or wanting to add their twopenn'orth about what's going on in Ambridge. They also perform wonders in juggling the availability of the actors with the needs of the writers' storylines.

I know many people often feel that we'd be better off without our bosses but that's not true. Good bosses are worth their weight in gold in the support and encouragement they can provide and, perhaps more importantly, in their readiness to let others get on with the job they're paid to do. We were delighted to have the company of the managing director of network radio, David Hatch; the controller of Radio 4, Michael Green; the head of broadcasting in the Midlands, David Waine; and the head of drama, John Tydeman.

The listeners ... it's trite to ask where would we be without them? But that doesn't diminish the truth of the answer: nowhere. Sometimes we might wish we could live in an ivory tower with doors that shut firmly against the world. It would be lovely to sit back and be judged only by one's own standards and not worry about what other people think. Luckily, our listeners won't let us do that. More than any other programme I know, *The Archers* is the listeners' programme. Their interest in what goes on in Ambridge is intense and they're never shy about telling us exactly what they think. Our 7½ million listeners were represented at the banquet by the five winners of a *Daily Mirror* competition and their partners.

There can't be too many BBC occasions when the Fourth Estate is unreservedly welcome, but the relationship between *The Archers* and the press has been consistently cordial and we were delighted to see some of the ladies and gentlemen of Fleet Street (or Wapping or Knightsbridge or wherever the spirits now reside) among our most welcome guests.

Tum-ti-tum-ti-tum ... Barwick Green, *as you've never heard it before, was performed by one of the country's top singing groups, Cantabile, for the ten thousandth episode celebration programme.*

Indeed, it was Gillian Reynolds, of the *Daily Telegraph*, who responded on behalf of all the guests. Gillian, who would be described as the doyenne of the national newspapers' radio correspondents if she were much older, is one of the programme's most enthusiastic – though often critical – listeners. On this occasion, however, she had come to praise *The Archers*.

She compared the attention given to the programme in the preceding week's newspapers with that of the news that the television soap, *Dynasty*, was to end after eight years. 'Isn't it amazing that 10 000 episodes of a radio serial should totally eclipse such a television event both on the printed page and in the hearts of the nation?'

Praise, yes, but there was still a nice acerbic touch when she referred to our promotional activities: 'Jock Gallagher, for once in his life, had absolutely no comment to make when I asked him whether Joan Collins, having killed Alexis off, is now free to come and manage The Bull . . . if and when, of course, Peggy decides to sell it!'

Gillian didn't know it at the time, but Niall Fraser, the programme's young producer, had come within an ace of booking Miss Collins for the special episode but negotiations had broken down because of her busy schedules. I wonder what the press would have made of that? If the reaction to Dame Edna's appearance was anything to go by, I suspect we would have come in for a fair amount of criticism.

On the night, however, there were no such thoughts in Gillian Reynolds' head:
It's been a privilege tonight to meet the founding fathers and founding mothers of **The Archers***, especially the woman [Valerie Shryane, then the programme's production assistant] who drew the original map to decide where everyone lived. And now we know where everyone lives – we live there, too, sometimes!*

The controller of Radio 4, Michael Green, proposed the toast to *The Archers* and was quick to show that he knew which side his bread was buttered in relation to the programme:
No self-respecting head of Radio 4 can afford to be unaware that even the good guys have trouble with their slurry! [At the time Philip Archer was having

trouble with his slurry getting into the Am.] Getting the omnibus fix on Sunday morning is crucial to the survival of anybody in this job.

To underline the historic nature of the celebrations, the controller had been digging in the archives to learn more about the genesis of the programme:
There was quite a lot of debate about the title, and I came across this note: 'At the moment the programme is under the name of the farm family but as the whole idea of the programme is to deal with a wider aspect of country life, I can see no reason why something like **Little Twittington** *wouldn't do as well.' What's in a name, indeed!*
Like Michael Green, I somehow don't think Little Twittington would have found the same place in the country's affections as Ambridge, nor do I think the original suggestion for Dan Archer's farm – Wimberton – would have had the same appeal as Brookfield.

When she spoke on behalf of the cast, June Spencer showed why she had been so popular as an after-dinner entertainer in the days before she joined *The Archers*. There was a distinct twinkle in her eye when she reflected on her character's romantic entanglement with the unseen, unheard Godfrey: 'Who knows, perhaps when Godfrey Wendover finally makes his appearance he will turn out, to Peggy's great delight, to be a toy boy!'

June, from whom most people *would* buy a secondhand car, then went on to comment on the programme's condition after more than 38 years:
We may be knocking on a bit but we're still young in spirit. It doesn't matter how many miles there are on the clock, it's the state of the engine and the bodywork that matters. Well, tomorrow we shall have 10 000 on the clock but I think our bodywork and our engine is in pretty good nick!

We were able to share a little of the occasion with listeners, in a special programme written and presented by Barry Norman as part of the evening's entertainment. It was broadcast on Radio 4 a couple of nights later. Barry, a long-time listener, talked about how *The Archers* had reached deep down into the British psyche:
It has touched that secret desire within us all to own 2 acres and a cow . . . this everyday story of

The wit and wisdom . . . Gillian Reynolds of the Daily Telegraph cast her critic's eye over the 10 000 episodes and pronounced most of them pretty good!

A night off . . . from the flicks for Barry Norman, from the scripts for PA Jane Froggatt, and from the trials and tribulations of editing the Radio Times for Nicholas Brett.

The entertaining Mrs Archer . . . June Spencer (right) turned the clock back when she once again became an after-dinner entertainer to respond to the Archers toast.

countryfolk that first shuffled on to the airwaves without much conviction and wearing an embarrassed grin on 1 January 1951, and which has stuck around ever since to become a cornerstone of British broadcasting.

Tonight we're gathered here at a star-studded banquet, a ploughman's lunch might be appropriate, but a banquet is what we've got – and who's complaining?

It's not . . . it is! Joe Grundy isn't sure whether the pain in his neck is from a tight tuxedo or from Lynda Snell's rabbiting on about how gorgeous – 'but not quite as nice as mine' – Zandra Rhodes' dress is.

Radio 1 raps the writers (top right) . . . John Walters' hilarious performance included a glorious rap poem chastising the scriptwriters for underplaying the Grundys.

Wait until they see this at The Cat and Fiddle . . . Eddie Grundy dressed up like a dog's dinner! Truth to tell, he's decided he can't beat 'em, so he's joined 'em. Here he is, trying hard to plug his latest record with the controller of Radio 1, Johnny Beerling.

Now this is a series that first started winning awards in the 1950s and made a habit of it. Today, rather greedily you might think, it holds the trophies not only for the best drama but also for the best contemporary programme on British radio. After 38 years that's not bad and, indeed, after 38 years it sits unchallenged in the **Guinness Book of Records** as the longest-running daily serial in the world.

I'm told that it's taken more than 30 million words to tell the story so far. Well, just think about that. It's the equivalent of five hundred average-length novels – or at least ten if you're talking about Jeffrey Archer though he, of course, is no relation.

While the Archers, the real Archers not Jeffrey, have been milking and ploughing, sowing and reaping and generally muck-spreading – not only on the farm but also in The Bull, where they must have downed about 30 million pints of Shires Bitter – Britain has seen some remarkable changes.

The programme began during the post-war years of depression and rationing, witnessed the coronation of a new young queen, the coming and going of eight prime ministers, and the coming if not yet the going of a ninth. It has seen the proliferation of nuclear weapons, the shrinking of the Empire, the formation of the Common Market, the arrival of commercial television.

A soap opera? Yes, **The Archers** is that but it's more than that. It is, in its own way, a fascinating chronicle of British life over nearly four decades and perhaps for that reason as much as for the bucolic escapism it offers, it has hooked and made addicts of millions of people.

This is not just a programme. This is a cult. The kind of people who would rather move house than lend so much as a cup of sugar to neighbours, get that dreamy look in their eyes whenever they hear **The Archers** signature tune!

I don't know whether or not she lends her neighbours sugar but Zandra Rhodes certainly had the dreamy look when she heard 'Barwick Green' sung by the group, Cantabile, and she picked up Barry Norman's cult theme when she put the programme alongside Alistair Cooke's *Letter from America* and *Gardeners' Question Time* as her favourites. It had, she said, irresistible pulling power for listeners:

In my own workroom, where I do my textile designing, the staff actually won't answer the phone to talk to me when I ring to ask them a question when **The Archers** *is on. It's very clever propaganda about the English countryside. I don't read enough and it's only by listening to the programme that I can make myself intelligent! It keeps one feeling very English.*

One of the highlights of the evening was a wonderful stand-up routine by Radio 1's John Walters. He's a member of the Eddie Grundy Fan Club and in a pop-style tribute to his hero, he produced 'The Archers Rap':

Now I know you writers have a difficult job
But I sometimes feel you feel that Eddie's just a yob.
He's weak in the head and not willing in the arm
But there's more to life than Brookfield Farm.
It's Archers, Archers all through the week
Looks as though Kenton'll be up before the Beak.
The Am's full of slurry, but Phil got off.
He's a magistrate himself and a bit of a toff.

Mark and Shula don't seem to be able,
Despite Martin Lambert saying up on the table.
Aldridge never meant a lot to me
But thanks to bovine spongiform encephalopathy
He's in the hospital holding his head
Married to an Archer he'd be better off dead.
I bet Peggy puts The Bull up for sale.
What about the drinkers? I hear you wail.
We're in The Cat and Fiddle knocking back the beers.
We're bored with The Archers and their 'opes and fears.
We Grundy fans couldn't get more fanner
But you still make the Archers lords of the manor.
When are the writers going to write
That episode that sets the wrongs to right,
That raises the programme to that wondrous height,
Of that magical moment and that glorious sight,
When Eddie was sick in the piana!

The Grundys, on their best behaviour, looked suitably abashed at such notoriety being thrust upon them and even Clarrie looked pleased!

Glenys Kinnock, wife of the Labour leader, was paying a return visit to *The Archers*, and she said her invitation to the banquet had been the envy of many of her friends. If they had been with her, however, there would have been an inevitable debate about whether the programme was better or worse than it used to be and about which character was the most lovable, pitiable or, indeed, intolerable:

The debate would grow increasingly heated as we slipped away from talking about a programme, and slipped into talking about Ambridge and its saints and sinners and snobs and poor souls as if they were actually in the room with us. Such is Ambridge-itis.

We all suffer from it and we all delight in it. It was the condition which David Blunkett (the Labour MP) diagnosed in himself recently when he called **The Archers** a silly soap opera and then later quickly said that of course nothing would ever stop him listening to it.

It isn't just the programme itself, it's a lot of other things. I think it is mainly the certainty factor.

There's no opposition from Glenys Kinnock . . . if the proposition is that The Archers *continues for another 10 000 episodes! She prefers it to television soap operas because the pictures are better.*

The knowledge that whatever turmoil exists in real life or even in politics – which is not always, of course, the same thing – **The Archers** can be turned on and all of a sudden you're covinced that, after all, everything is going to be all right.

Then there is what we all feel after the programme, a sort of afterglow. You're left musing on the questions that they leave hanging in the air (and I must admit to being an omnibus listener, not an evening one), questions that would, I think, perplex the oracle at Delphi. For instance, why is it I keep asking myself that Pat, my compatriot, who turned from being a feminist and a progressive who threatened to really churn up that placid rural scene, is now very seriously dedicating her fervour and her thinking powers to being, of all things, a yoghurt tycoon?

Why is it that Mike Tucker was the only farmer that I or, indeed, any of you have ever heard of who ever went bankrupt? I ask myself, was it because he was, and is, so cantankerous and taciturn or because he was an activist in the Transport and General Workers Union, Agricultural Workers Sections?

I ask what moral lesson do we draw from his insolvency and why is Ambridge the only place in Britain where no passing sound, no conversation, no breeze over a field ever carries even any sound of anyone talking about **Coronation Street**, **EastEnders**, **Dallas** or **Neighbours**? How refreshing that is.

These are, I think, the real questions of our age. They bother many, including one of the most **Archers**-resistant people I know . . . my husband. The man who claims that he never listens to **The Archers** but somehow always seems to have enough textual knowledge to be extremely irritated by Elizabeth (I think that he actually sees shades of Rachel Kinnock in her. And they are, in fact, very similar!); to call for a popular uprising against Jack Woolley; and to think so much of Joe and Eddie Grundy that he actually wants the programme retitled **The Grundys and Their Oppressors**, an everyday story of how the anarchists overthrew the dictatorship of the Green Welly Brigade.

Frankly, I have to say that if the writers and the producers and the actors on the programme were to be paid on a tonnage basis – paid according to the size of their audience – their fees should be doubled to account for all the people who insist that they **never** listen to **The Archers**.

On behalf of them in the outer circle, as it were, and all of us in the inner circle of true self-confessed addicts, I say long may **The Archers** continue . . . to its two millionth edition and beyond.

We all agree with that little girl who when asked why she liked radio answered: 'It's so much nicer than TV, the pictures are better.' Please, please, everyone in **The Archers**, keep the pictures coming!

Mrs Kinnock's exhortation fell on highly receptive ears. There are certainly more pictures where the last 10 000 came from.

CHAPTER TEN

ACCOLADES

WE WOULD SAY *The Archers* was pretty wonderful, wouldn't we? so it's nice that so many other people have said it for us . . . in so many different ways and over so many years. Accolades, formal and informal, have been showered on the programme to reinforce its place in the affections of the listeners.

From its early days, *The Archers* was recognised as having special qualities. Within the first year, it had outstripped *Mrs Dale's Diary* in terms of popularity. The old *Daily Graphic* carried out an opinion poll in 1952 in which nearly 80 per cent of readers voted for the everyday story of countryfolk. A year later, *Reveille* readers named it the second most popular show on radio and by 1953, the *Daily Mail* Award for the most entertaining programme was safely in Tony Shryane's hands.

The *Radio Times* has been one of Britain's most successful and popular magazines for many years and, such is the competition, only the top programmes and artistes are likely to be featured on the famous front cover. *The Archers* was given the prime spot as early as November 1951, and it has continued to win its place there regularly. In recent years, the magazine has featured Lord Lichfield's photograph of Shula, the bride, as well as Terry Wogan and some of the cast celebrating the ten thousandth episode.

Another test of the programme's popularity is the amount that's been written about it. We've already commented on the press coverage but equally impressive is the number of books that have been written about life in Ambridge. Each one bought is an accolade for the programme as well as the author.

While the list doesn't quite match the prolific achievements of the scriptwriters who (as Barry Norman pointed out) have written the equivalent of 500 full-length novels, the bibliography of *The Archers* makes interesting reading in itself:

The Archers of Ambridge (novel)
by Edward J. Mason and Geoffrey Webb, 1955

Doris Archer's Farm Cookbook
by Gwen Berryman, 1958

The Archers Intervene (novel)
by Edward J. Mason and Geoffrey Webb, 1960

Peggy Archer's Book of Recipes
BBC, 1968

Doris Archer's 21-Year Diary
by Jock Gallagher, 1971

Doris Archer's Ambridge Diary
by Jock Gallagher, 1972

The Archers . . . a Slice of My Life
(autobiography) by Godfrey Baseley, 1973

Ambridge Summer (novel)
by Keith Miles, 1975

Brookfield Spring (novel)
by Brian Hayles, 1975

Forever Ambridge (autobiography)
by Norman Painting, 1975

Twenty-five Years of The Archers
by Jock Gallagher, 1975

Tom Forrest's Country Calendar
by Charles Lefeaux, 1978

The Archers: The First Thirty Years
by William Smethurst, 1980

Ambridge: An English Village Through the Ages by Jennifer Aldridge and John Tregorran,
William Smethurst, 1982

The Life and Death of Doris Archer
(autobiography) by Gwen Berryman, 1982

Dan Archer: The Ambridge Years
by William Smethurst, 1984

The Archers Official Companion
by William Smethurst, 1986

To the Victor the Spoils, Return to Ambridge and *Borchester Echoes* (novels)
by Jock Gallagher, 1988

The Archers Quizbook
by Liz Rigbey, 1988

The Archers Book of Farming and the Countryside
by Anthony Parkin, 1989

Even this is far from being a comprehensive list. It includes only those books known to the present production staff and any information readers may have about other books would be very welcome.

Almost as important as the public acclaim is the acknowledgement of professionalism by one's peers and, here, the programme staff are certainly entitled to feel pleased. Over the years, *The Archers* has won every possible award . . . two *Daily Mail* Awards in the 1950s and another two in 1988; two Writers' Guild prizes in the 1960s; the old Pye Radio Award in the 1970s; and in the 1980s we struck gold!

In 1987, *The Archers* became the first programme to win the Sony Gold Award. Until then, radio's premier award had always gone to individuals. In 1988, the programme was added to the Sony 'Roll of Honour' and the *Daily Mail* again polled its readers to determine the favourite radio programmes of the day. Not altogether unexpectedly, *The Archers* was voted the best drama programme. Everyone, however, was very surprised – and delighted – when we were also voted the best contemporary programme on the radio. To win such an award after more than 37 years of broadcasting was an astonishing achievement.

The first of *The Archers'* royal accolades came in 1961, when, in the Queen's Birthday Honours, Tony Shryane was appointed an MBE for his services to broadcasting and received his award from the Queen Mother. While Tony, modest and generous as ever, said the honour should be shared by everyone concerned with the programme's production, it was quite clear that it was a personal accolade. No one deserved it more. He had produced every single episode over those first ten years.

During the awards ceremony, the Queen Mother had intimated to Tony that the programme was one of her firm favourites and when, ten years later, her granddaughter, Princess Anne, came to see *The Archers* being produced at the Pebble Mill

This time it's silver . . . June Spencer accepts the Daily Mail's silver microphone from managing director Alwyn Robinson after a 1988 poll of readers voted The Archers *the best contemporary programme on radio. The discerning readers also made it the best drama and awarded a second silver microphone.*

Going for gold . . . Roy Hudd presents the Sony Gold Award to Jock Gallagher at a ceremony in the Grosvenor House Hotel, London, in 1987. The award was to mark the outstanding contribution to broadcasting by the cast and production team.

studios in Birmingham, we returned the compliment. The visit coincided with the build-up to the twenty-first anniversary celebrations and we had a special medallion minted for the occasion. We had one made in solid gold and asked the Princess to accept it on the Queen Mother's behalf.

Norman Painting was next to appear in the Honours List . . . in 1976, when the programme celebrated its silver jubilee. Norman was also honoured by the Royal Agricultural Society of England, by being elected the society's only honorary governor. It was a very good time for him because the previous year he had published his autobiography, *Forever Ambridge*, and it had got into the bestseller lists.

Five years later, Gwen Berryman became the first woman to be named Midlander of the Year and that proved to be a precursor to her also being appointed an MBE as the programme celebrated 30 years on the air. In 1984, Chriss Gittins became the fourth member of the team to go to Buckingham Palace. He received his medal from the Queen and brought back the eagerly awaited news: Her Majesty was one of our listeners!

Photographer royal . . . Weddings can be a very serious business for one of the country's top professionals, Lord Lichfield. His efficiency and charm won over all the guests at Shula and Mark's wedding, although Jethro Larkin found it all a bit hard on the feet!

By Royal Appointment . . . Episode 8715 is recorded at Kensington Palace (doubling on this occasion as Grey Gables), where HRH Princess Margaret became the first member of the Royal Family to join the cast of a soap opera. In her own drawing room she played a scene opposite Sara Coward (Caroline Bone) and Arnold Peters (Jack Woolley). There is now a Royal Garden Suite at Grey Gables in case HRH decides to visit again!

Perhaps the greatest royal acknowledgement of *The Archers'* unique role in British life was Princess Margaret's readiness to appear on the programme. It was the first and, so far, the last time a member of the Royal Family has appeared in a soap opera.

Lord Lichfield only accepted the commission to take the wedding photographs because he is such an enthusiastic fan of the programme. He has been known to complain bitterly to the BBC World Service about why it isn't broadcast all round the world.

The Duke of Westminster enjoyed his appearance on the programme so much that he later sent a note in which he said he hoped Jack Woolley would get a knighthood for sponsoring the Ambridge Festival.

In 1988, the Princess Royal was president of

the Royal Agricultural Society of England and it was Her Royal Highness who presented us with a framed citation recording:

The great achievement of the British Broadcasting Corporation in improving understanding of countryside matters and country life through the medium of **The Archers** *since 1951.*

The programme produced by the BBC in the Midlands has made a significant contribution to the progress of agriculture in the United Kingdom and worldwide.

In 1989, the Prime Minister spoke about her interest in the programme first in a magazine interview and then in a letter to the producers:

Over the years it has faithfully reflected changes in farming practice in well-developed storylines. A recent example has been the set-aside scheme. In

Your estate or mine? Ambridge's major landowner, Jack Woolley, meets the Duke of Westminster, one of the country's biggest landowners, when he visits Grey Gables for a fashion gala in aid of the NSPCC. The Duke's visit was arranged by Caroline Bone, an old family friend, and it coincided with his chairmanship of the charity's centenary appeal. It is not recorded how much Mr Woolley donated.

1984, when Tony and Pat Archer took the adventurous step of converting to organic farming, **The Archers** *was in the forefront of the movement.*

This everyday story of countryfolk has had its share of disasters with foot and mouth disease in 1956 and fowl pest in 1960. Practical advice on how to cope was woven into the dialogue. BST in milk and BSE are issues which have been tackled recently and conservation measures are now regularly discussed.

Taking umbrage . . . Eddie Grundy teamed up with The Federation for an assault on the Top Twenty. The hit parade hit back and Eddie continues to live in hope of fame and fortune.

In all these areas, **The Archers** has remained true to the best standards of British broadcasting, seeking always to inform, educate and entertain. Above all else, the reason for its success and longevity has been the strength of its main characters and the rich continuity of family life which they represent.

There are, I hope, more accolades to come, and more prizes to be won. If so, they will bring a sense of satisfaction and a feeling of being loved that will help to cushion the blows that are also inevitably waiting around the corner.

With the programme team refreshed and full of youthful energy and commitment, there are no immediate dangers; indeed there are no problems I can see even on the far horizon. Anything that comes along now can only be a minor setback. *The Archers* is set fair for another 10 000 episodes.

161